FOREST DIPLOMACY

Cultures in Conflict on the Pennsylvania Frontier, 1757

REACTING CONSORTIUM

OTHER TITLES IN THIS SERIES

Red Clay, 1835: Cherokee Removal and the Meaning of Sovereignty
Jace Weaver and Laura Adams Weaver
The Constitutional Convention of 1787: Constructing the American Republic
John Patrick Coby
Kentucky, 1861: Loyalty, State, and Nation
Nicolas W. Proctor and Margaret Storey
Greenwich Village, 1913: Suffrage, Labor, and the New Woman
Mary Jane Treacy
Patriots, Loyalists, and Revolution in New York City, 1775–1776, Second Edition
Bill Offutt
Rousseau, Burke, and Revolution in France, 1791, Second Edition
Jennifer Popiel, Mark C. Carnes, and Gary Kates
The Threshold of Democracy: Athens in 403 BCE, Fourth Edition
Josiah Ober, Naomi J. Norman, and Mark C. Carnes

Also Available

Charles Darwin, the Copley Medal, and the Rise of Naturalism, 1861–1864
Marsha Driscoll, Elizabeth E. Dunn, Dann Siems, and B. Kamran Swanson
Confucianism and the Succession Crisis of the Wanli Emperor, 1587
Daniel K. Gardner and Mark C. Carnes
Defining a Nation: India on the Eve of Independence, 1945
Ainslie T. Embree and Mark C. Carnes
The Trial of Anne Hutchinson: Liberty, Law, and Intolerance in Puritan New England
Michael P. Winship and Mark C. Carnes
The Trial of Galileo: Aristotelianism, the "New Cosmology," and the Catholic Church, 1616–1633
Michael S. Pettersen, Frederick Purnell, Jr., and Mark C. Carnes

FOREST DIPLOMACY

Cultures in Conflict on the Pennsylvania Frontier, 1757

Nicolas W. Proctor, Simpson College

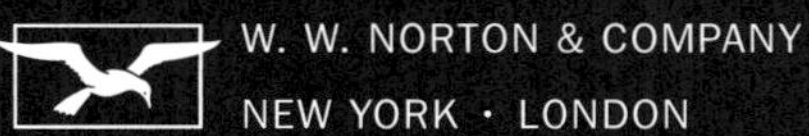

BARNARD
REACTING TO THE PAST

W. W. Norton & Company has been independent since its founding in 1923, when William Warder Norton and Mary D. Herter Norton first published lectures delivered at the People's Institute, the adult education division of New York City's Cooper Union. The firm soon expanded its program beyond the Institute, publishing books by celebrated academics from America and abroad. By midcentury, the two major pillars of Norton's publishing program—trade books and college texts—were firmly established. In the 1950s, the Norton family transferred control of the company to its employees, and today—with a staff of four hundred and a comparable number of trade, college, and professional titles published each year—W. W. Norton & Company stands as the largest and oldest publishing house owned wholly by its employees.

Editor: Justin Cahill
Project Editor: Caitlin Moran
Assistant Editor: Rachel Taylor
Managing Editor, College: Marian Johnson
Production Manager: Stephen Sajdak
Marketing Manager, History: Sarah England Bartley
Design Director: Rubina Yeh
Book Design: Alexandra Charitan
Permissions Manager: Megan Schindel
Composition: Jouve North America
Cartographer: Mapping Specialists, Ltd.
Manufacturing: Sheridan Books

ISBN: 978-0-393-67378-4

W. W. Norton & Company, Inc., 500 Fifth Avenue, New York, NY 10110
W. W. Norton & Company Ltd., 15 Carlisle Street, London W1D 3BS

ABOUT THE AUTHOR

NICOLAS W. PROCTOR is professor of history at Simpson College. He received his Ph.D. in U.S. history from Emory University and is the author of *Bathed in Blood: Hunting and Mastery in the Old South*. He is also the chair of the Reacting to the Past editorial board, and the author of Reacting games on the Seven Years' War on the Pennsylvania frontier, the Chicago Democratic Convention of 1968, Reconstruction in New Orleans, and the art of the Paris Exposition Universelle of 1889, as well as a handbook for Reacting game designers.

CONTENTS

Pennsylvania's Land Claims, 1737–1754

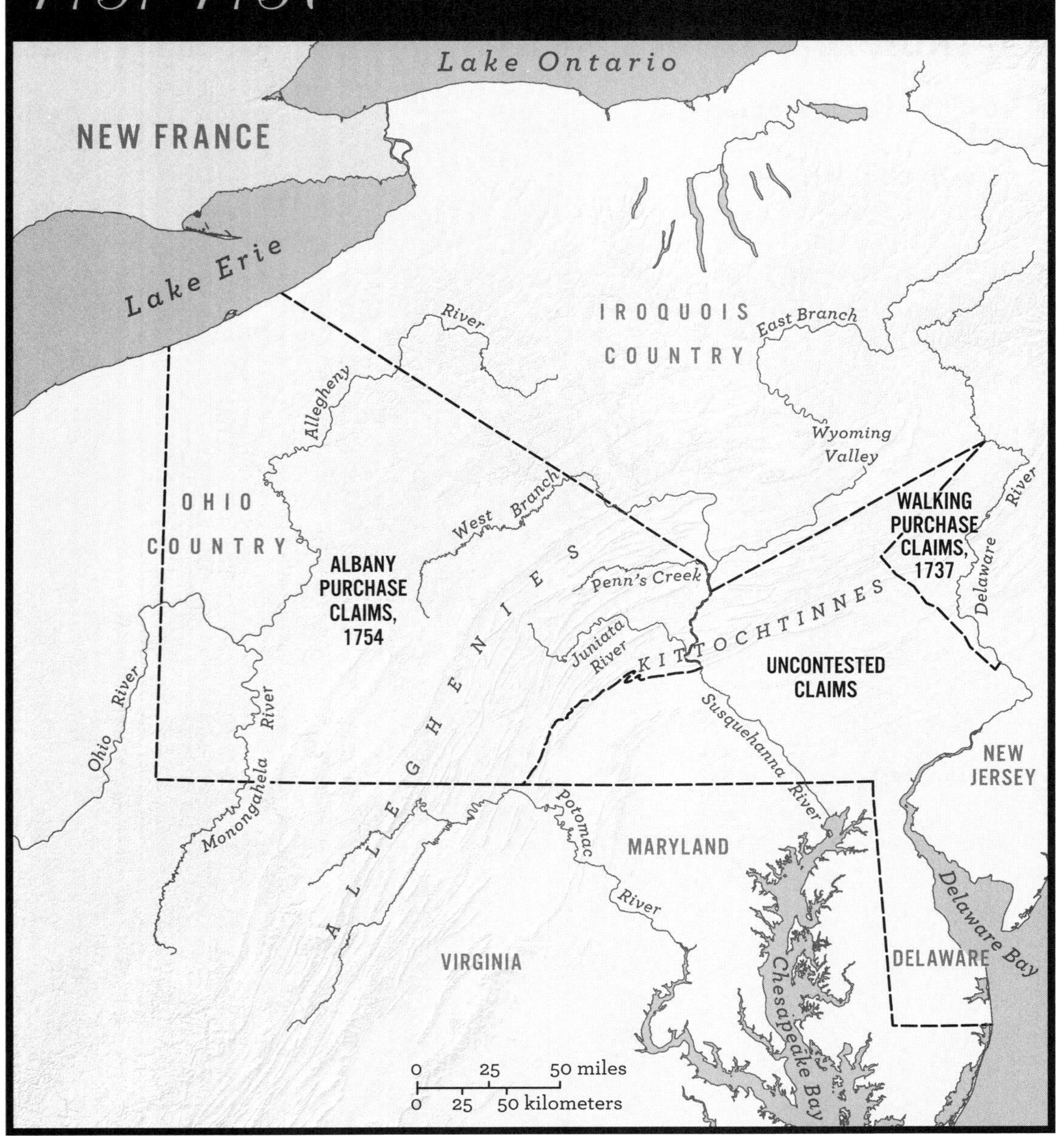

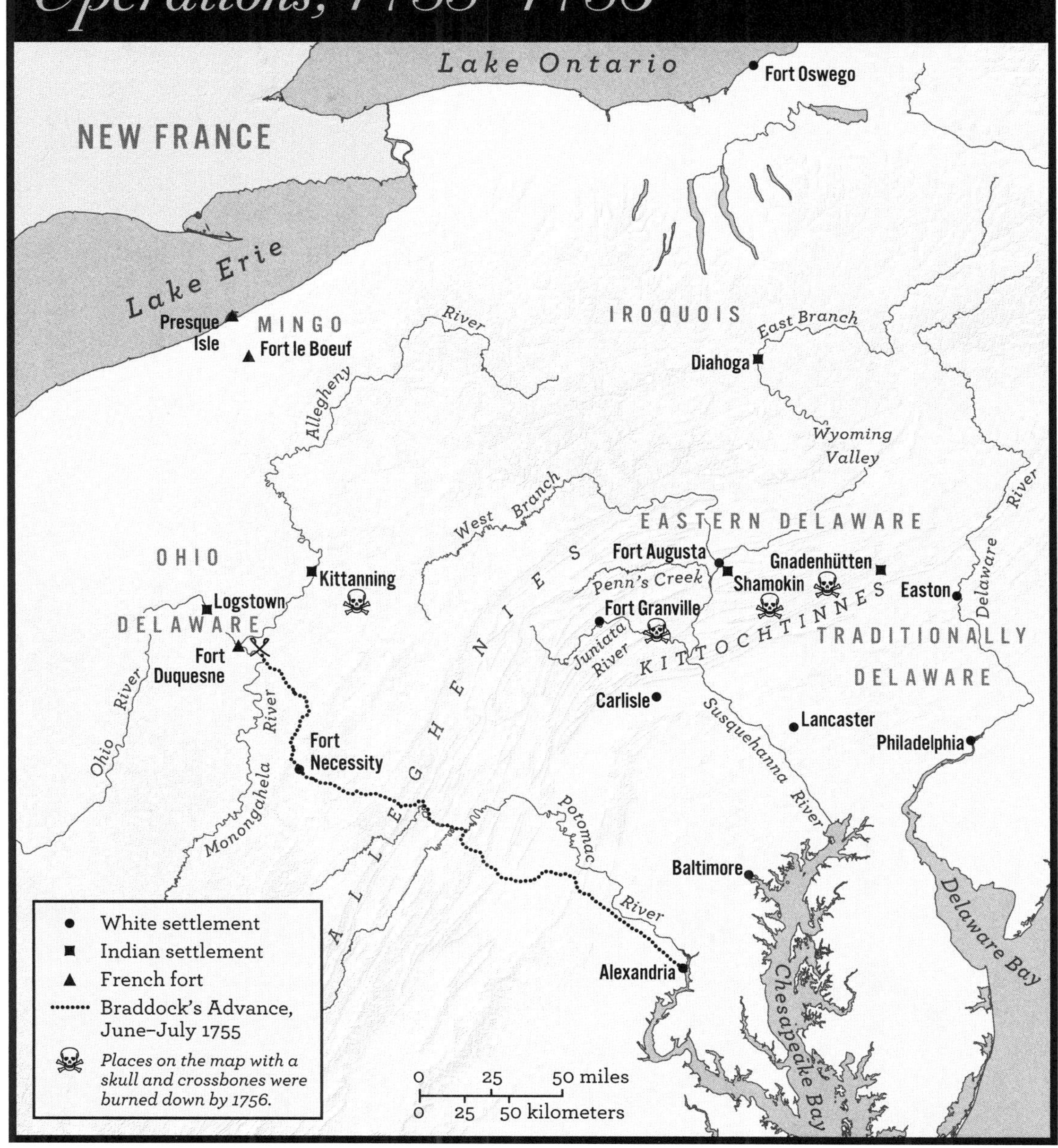
Major Settlements and Military Operations, 1755–1756
Lake Ontario
Fort Oswego
NEW FRANCE
Lake Erie
Presque Isle
MINGO
Fort le Boeuf
River
IROQUOIS
East Branch
Diahoga
Allegheny
Wyoming Valley
West Branch
River
EASTERN DELAWARE
OHIO
Kittanning
Fort Augusta
Gnadenhütten
Shamokin
Penn's Creek
Easton
Logstown
Fort Granville
Delaware
DELAWARE
Juniata River
KITTOCHTINNES
TRADITIONALLY DELAWARE
Fort Duquesne
ALLEGHENIES
River
Ohio River
Carlisle
Monongahela River
Susquehanna River
Lancaster
Philadelphia
Fort Necessity
Potomac River
Baltimore
Delaware Bay
Alexandria
Chesapeake Bay
White settlement
Indian settlement
French fort
Braddock's Advance, June–July 1755
Places on the map with a skull and crossbones were burned down by 1756.
0 25 50 miles
0 25 50 kilometers

PART 1: INTRODUCTION

BRIEF OVERVIEW OF THE GAME

Forest Diplomacy begins as the European settlers in colonial Pennsylvania and the Delaware Indians (or Lenâpé) are engaged in a vicious and destructive war. This conflict will eventually merge with the global mid-eighteenth century struggle between Britain and France known in Europe as the Seven Years' War and in the United States as the French and Indian War. The focus of the game is a treaty council in 1757, which seeks to end the conflict on the frontier. Before the game begins, players will explore the historical context, previous treaties, firsthand accounts of the war, controversies over Quaker pacifism, and various Iroquois and Delaware cultural texts. Once the game begins players will negotiate with one another in an attempt to hammer out a broadly acceptable treaty. After the game ends, there is an opportunity for debriefing and reflection. The game itself is divided into three distinct phases.

Prelude

Players divide into three groups: Interpreters, Pennsylvanians, and Indians. The latter two groups meet separately from one another, but Interpreters may shuttle back and forth. This gives players an opportunity to identify with their assigned cultures. It also allows distrust and suspicion to fester.

Treaty Council

Players reunite when formal treaty deliberations begin. The structure of these meetings is dictated by the traditional rituals of eastern woodland Indian diplomacy, which are intended to create a dispassionate space in the midst of the bloodthirstiness of war. Understanding the attendant cultural conventions becomes an essential element in peacemaking, which can be difficult given the divineness of issues like scalping, the liquor trade, captive taking, cultural assimilation, and the seizure of land.

Coda

When negotiations conclude, players must attempt to uphold whatever agreements they forged in the Treaty Council. If the treaty remains disagreeable to a significant number of participants, it will collapse amid renewed violence. However, if enough participants can be convinced that the treaty represents a just peace then it will stand.

PROLOGUE: THREE ROADS TO EASTON

A Lenâpé Seeking Justice

The path you follow is a familiar one. You have walked it many times before.

You were born in your people's ancestral homeland in the Delaware River valley, but when you were a boy, the women of your village made a momentous decision: it was time to leave. Your entire village crossed the Kittochtinny Hills and settled on the banks of the Susquehanna River in the town of Shamokin, which sheltered a variety of people who had been displaced by the whites.

The site of the colonial era settlement of Shamokin is now the city of Sunbury, Pennsylvania.

This meant that in addition to your own kin, you grew up among people who considered themselves Conoy, Shawnee, Nanticoke, and Mahican. In time, intermarriage, adoption, familiarity, and political necessity began to meld many of these peoples together into a collection of peoples who came to be known as the Delawares.

There were also those who held themselves apart. Foremost among them were those who belonged to the peoples of the Iroquois League: the Haudenosaunee. In time, the whites followed you across the hills. A handful of white traders made their homes in Shamokin. Some of these men were good, but many were filled with greed and deceitfulness. You decided that you would not trade with them.

After you became an accomplished hunter, you and some friends followed the path back across the Kittochtinnes with a pack of deerskins and beaver pelts. You traded them with white men near the rising village of Easton for metal tools, cloth, liquor, powder, and lead. The land where you were born was changing before your eyes. You watched as the whites broke the land to their will, clearing trees, piling stones into walls, and gouging the earth in long strips with their cattle and their plows.

During this visit, some white men spoke about their god. They promised great rewards for those who wore white men's uncomfortable shoes, ate their food, and lived in their cold, damp houses. Some listened and stayed with the whites, but you were unimpressed and returned to Shamokin.

Soon, white families started building farms nearby. Their hogs rooted in your fields. They scared the deer away. They plied your people with liquor and insisted that they owned the land they farmed because they had bought it from powerful whites—*the Proprietors*—who lived far away across the ocean in England. These Proprietors were the sons of William Penn. You remembered him as a friend of Indians, but you did not know his sons. No one seemed to know the sons.

These claims of ownership confused you, so you asked a white trader how these "Proprietors" had come to own the land, land that, you pointed out, you had lived on for most of your life. He answered simply: they bought it from the Iroquois.

Everyone knew that the nations of the Haudenosaunee considered your people (and all of the other peoples who lived in Shamokin) their subordinates, but you did not understand how this arrogant presumption extended to the sale and ownership of land. Some Iroquois lived in Shamokin, but they were in the minority. From time to time their war parties descended the Susquehanna River from the Iroquois lands to the north. They passed through Shamokin on their journey to make war on southern peoples like the Catawbas and Cherokee, but they never farmed the land and rarely hunted in its forests. The authority of the league seemed distant and indistinct. There was an Iroquois chief named Shickellamy who observed the happenings in Shamokin and reported them back to the Grand Council of the Haudenosaunee in Onondaga, but he had died years ago. All of this led to a second question: Why did the Iroquois think they owned the land?

The answer came quickly again, for the trader was a clever man, well versed in the ways of Indians: the Iroquois had defeated the Susquehannock in a great war. The land was theirs by right of conquest.

This quick and simple answer failed to clarify matters in your mind. Old people told you that a people called the Susquehannock once lived along the Susquehanna River valley in great numbers. Some of their descendants live there still and are called Conestoga, while others were apparently adopted into the longhouses of the Iroquois, but it is difficult to be certain about any of this because the Iroquois conquest of the Susquehannock allegedly occurred in your grandfather's grandfather's time. Even if these stories were true, what, you wondered, do they have to do with the status of the land today?

By this point the trader had tired of your questions. He encouraged you to take a drink of rum. You obliged him. Then you obliged him again. And again. A few hours later, you traded him an entire year's worth of deerskins for some old blankets and a small pot with a hole in the bottom. When you returned home your wife shamed you utterly. Her mother and the other women in the longhouse refused to speak with you for months. The eyes of your children glittered with contempt and resentment.

Your shame hobbled you until war came. War began in earnest with a great victory by the French and their Indian allies over the British army under the command of General Braddock, who arrogantly marched deep into the woods at the head of his redcoats and a rabble of colonials. The French knew the ways of the woods better. They waited, and when they sprang their trap they destroyed Braddock's army. This tore apart the most peaceful frontier in North America. Encouraged by the potential for regaining a measure of your personal honor, you joined a raiding party. Other Delaware joined too.

You laid an ambush in the Kittochtinnes near where you walk today. You did not wait for long before spotting a small party of refugees struggling toward the safety of Philadelphia. You were surprised and gratified to see the trader who dishonored you among them. When the trap was sprung and the first shots rang out, he ran. You brought him to bay at the foot of a towering elm. Even though he did not recognize your face under the black paint, you experienced some satisfaction when you split open his skull and removed his scalp.

That was a year ago. The war spread quickly, and the once laughably inept whites have started striking out with raids of their own. To escape their depredations, you helped your family move into the southern reaches of Haudenosaunee country at Diahoga. They are cold and hungry. Few crops were planted last spring, and war parties have little time for hunting. The French are no help. They barely have enough to feed themselves even at their big fort—Fort Duquesne—in the Ohio Country. The women feel this hardship keenly. The matriarch of the longhouse gave you clear instructions before you set out for this council: make peace and make it now.

Now you prepare to follow the well-trod path to Easton and the land of your ancestors. You feel the weight of the flintlock in your hand and remember the trader who used liquor to make you drunk, impoverished, and ashamed in the course of a few hours. His death provided some compensation, but what of the years of indignity brought by rooting hogs, deceitful surveyors, and the lying treachery of white men? The words of the matriarch carry great weight, but peace will not come without justice.

A Commissioner Seeking Peace

As your coach struggles northward along the rutted and muddy road you recall your first journey to the forest. As a boy, the streets of Philadelphia and the bountiful farms that surrounded it were very familiar. You cannot remember a time when you did not know them, but you do remember when you knew nothing of the wilderness that lay beyond. You were ten the first time your father took you outside the tight grid of streets and the orderly bounded fields of wheat and Indian corn. You had been in woods before—five-acre woodlots and wispy willow thickets along the streambeds—but this was different.

Then, as now, the Proprietors of Pennsylvania controlled all land purchases from the Indians. Therefore, they controlled the subsequent sale of those lands to Pennsylvanians. Fortunately, your father, a prosperous merchant, cultivated a number of well-connected acquaintances who informed him when particularly choice lots came up for sale.

One fine day you and he set out to examine a recent purchase. Passing out of settled country you guided your horses to follow what you took to be a deer path. You both became quiet beneath the towering dark eminence of ancient oaks, chestnuts, and walnuts, their trunks scorched black by ancient fires. Beneath the dense canopy of leaves, you both dismounted and began to look for blazes corresponding to the boundaries of the claim. Stooping through a dense tangle of bushes you lost your bearings and became separated from your father. Bewildered, you wandered deeper into the woods. You were swallowed up by dark green leaves. Darkness fell. Your cries went unheard. He did not find you until morning, cold and shivering.

The forest remained terrifying, but as you grew older, you saw that your father was right about one thing: there was money in it. Land speculation requires both capital and connections. Your family had both. Buying land from the Proprietary and selling it to German and Scots-Irish immigrants became a good business.

Sometimes Indians objected to these transactions, but you thought little of it as settlers swept westward. Knots of trees and clumps of Indians remained in their wake, but the tide seemed irresistible. Farms and pastures replaced the wild forest of your youth. Settlements carried all the way to the foot of the mountains and seemed prepared to wash over them and into the Ohio Country beyond. And the profits rolled in. Then, war came.

War has wrecked your business and flushed the streets of Philadelphia with angry refugees clamoring for Indian scalps. Trade has ground to a halt. Land sales have ceased. The French and their Indian allies menace the frontier. None of this is good, so you plan to strive for peace, but it cannot be peace at any price. It must not imperil your wealth or future prosperity.

The coach jolts and brings you back to the present. You glance at your fellow commissioners of the assembly. Together, as elected representatives of the Pennsylvania legislature, you represent the will of the freemen of Pennsylvania, but your peers do not appear confident or commanding now. Even the renowned Benjamin Franklin seems distant and unfocused. Perhaps he too is remembering past sojourns in the wilderness. Or, maybe, he is thinking about the Indians, for they are the reason you are preparing for a journey to the treaty council up the river at Easton.

Until last year you rarely thought about Indians. You occasionally saw a small group of them, at a distance, pursuing some obscure errand in Philadelphia, and you heard about Christian Indians peacefully living with German missionaries at settlements like Gnadenhütten, but you never met one in person. You never had a reason to.

You know your fine Philadelphia home sits on land purchased from the Lenâpé Indians by William Penn seventy or so years ago. He went so far as to buy the whole area several times over to satisfy his Quaker desires for honest dealing and peace. These efforts apparently succeeded, for you have never seen or heard from any of their descendants. Recent land deals have been less circumspect, but you accept this as the price of progress.

Indians are a cipher for you, yet over the years you have drafted and signed hundreds of documents that shape their lives. You have bought and sold land they believe to be theirs with the stroke of a pen. As a member of the assembly, you recently voted funding for scalp bounties, building forts, and arming a militia. As a result, Indians died. In many ways, you have been waging a war against them with paper for most of your adult life, but you have yet to look an Indian in the eye. Soon, you will.

A Quaker Pariah

You have attended numerous treaty negotiations as a representative of the Proprietors of Pennsylvania. A member of the Governor's Council, you are an old hand at Pennsylvania politics and the intrigues of forest diplomacy. And yet, you are ill at ease. Your faith is chafing.

As a Quaker you are committed to the peaceable testimony of the Society of Friends. Peace is the way of the Savior, so it should be the way of those who follow Him. William Penn's legacy once made this an easy path to follow, but now, war has come to Penn's woods.

This is not like when Britain fought France in King George's War. Then, the battles were far from Pennsylvania. Motivated by greed and ambition, it was a war of empire. Consequently, you quietly supported the efforts of the Quaker-dominated assembly to keep Pennsylvania from becoming drawn into the senseless bloodletting. Your prayers were answered when peace came, but faith must be tested, so war has come again: this time as a storm from the west. Two years ago the French and their Indian allies annihilated Braddock's army as it approached Fort Duquesne. Then, spurred on by French provocateurs, Indians began to fall upon the frontier settlers.

Seduced by French promises, deprived of English presents, and (you are honest with yourself about this now) upset about some questionable land purchases, the Indians have poured their wrath on the frontier settlers. Last winter, the raids escalated into a full-scale campaign to drive in the frontier. Farms once stretched from here to the Susquehanna Valley, but now Philadelphia teems with angry refugees as raiding parties roam unchecked through the countryside.

In the face of these assaults, you changed your position on military appropriations and advocated armed self-defense. This earned you the ire of purist Friends like John Woolman and Israel Pemberton. By supporting the arming of the militia, the construction of forts, and the payment of scalp bounties, you became a so-called defense Quaker. Once, other Friends saw you as a moderating influence on the Governor's Council. You moved easily in Philadelphia society and enjoyed a wide circle of acquaintances. Now, you are a pariah. The Philadelphia Meeting rebuked you. Friends ignore you in the street. You have tried to explain your reasoning and the direction provided by your inner light, but they refuse to listen. They severed you from their body.

This is a painful separation, yet as you prepare for your journey up the river to Easton, you believe it is one you must endure in the cause of peace.

HOW TO REACT

Reacting to the Past is a series of historical role-playing games. After a few preparatory lectures, the game begins and the students are in charge. Set in moments of heightened historical tension, the games place students in the roles of historical figures. By reading the game book and their individual role sheets, students discover their objectives, potential allies, and the forces that stand between them and victory. They must then attempt to achieve victory through formal speeches, informal debate, negotiations, and (sometimes) conspiracy. Outcomes sometimes part from actual history; a postmortem session sets the record straight.

The following is an outline of what you will encounter in Reacting and what you will be expected to do.

Game Setup

Your instructor will spend some time before the beginning of the game helping you understand the historical context for the game. During the setup period, you will use several different kinds of materials:

- The game book (from which you are reading now), which includes historical information, rules and elements of the game, and essential documents

- Your instructor will provide you with a role sheet, which includes a short biography of the historical figure you will model in the game as well as that person's ideology, objectives, responsibilities, and resources. Your role may be an actual historical figure or a composite.

In addition to the game book, you may also be required to read historical documents or books written by historians. These provide additional information and arguments for use during the game.

Read all of this contextual material and all of these documents and sources before the game begins. And just as important, go back and reread these materials throughout the game. A second and third reading while *in role* will deepen your understanding and alter your perspective, because ideas take on a different aspect when seen through the eyes of a partisan actor.

Students who have carefully read the materials and who know the rules of the game will invariably do better than those who rely on general impressions and uncertain memories.

Game Play

Once the game begins, class sessions are presided over by students. In most cases, a single student serves as a kind of presiding officer. The instructor then becomes the Gamemaster (GM) and takes a seat in the back of the room. Though he or she will not lead the class sessions, the GM may do any of the following:

- Pass notes
- Announce important events, some of which may be the result of student actions; others are instigated by the GM
- Redirect proceedings that have gone off track

The presiding officer is expected to observe basic standards of fairness, but as a fail-safe device, most Reacting to the Past games employ the "Podium Rule," which allows a student who has not been recognized to approach the podium and wait for a chance to speak. Once at the podium, the student has the floor and must be heard.

Role sheets contain private, secret information which students are expected to guard. You are advised, therefore, to exercise caution when discussing your role with others. Your role sheet probably identifies likely allies, but even they may not always be trustworthy. However, keeping your own counsel, or saying nothing to anyone, is not an option. To achieve your objectives, you *must* speak with others. You will never muster the voting strength to prevail without allies. Collaboration and coalition building are at the heart of every game.

These discussions must lead to action, which often means proposing, debating, and passing legislation. Someone therefore must be responsible for introducing the measure and explaining its particulars. And always remember that a Reacting game is only a game—resistance, attack, and betrayal are not to be taken personally, since game opponents are merely acting as their roles direct.

Some games feature strong alliances called *factions*; these are tight-knit groups with fixed objectives. Games with factions all include roles called Indeterminates or Independents. They operate outside of the established factions. They are not all entirely neutral; some are biased on certain issues. If you are in a faction, cultivating these players is in your interest, because they can be convinced to support your position. If you are lucky enough to have drawn one of these roles you should be pleased; you will likely play a pivotal role in the outcome of the game.

Game Requirements

Students in Reacting games practice persuasive writing, public speaking, critical thinking, teamwork, negotiation, problem solving, collaboration, adapting to changing circumstances, and working under pressure to meet deadlines. Your instructor will explain the specific requirements for your class. In general, though, a Reacting game asks you to perform three distinct activities:

Reading and Writing. This standard academic work is carried on more purposefully in a Reacting course, because what you read is put to immediate use and what you write is meant to persuade others to act the way you want them to. The reading load may have slight variations from role to role; the writing requirement depends on your particular course. Papers are often policy statements, but they can also be autobiographies, battle plans, spy reports, newspapers, poems, or after-game reflections. Papers provide the foundation for the speeches delivered in class.

Public Speaking and Debate. In the course of a game, almost everyone is expected to deliver at least one formal speech from the podium (the length of the game and the size of the class will determine the number of speeches). Debate follows. Debate can be impromptu, raucous, and fast paced and results in decisions voted on by the body. Gamemasters may stipulate that students must deliver their papers from memory when at the podium or may insist that students wean themselves from dependency on written notes as the game progresses.

Wherever the game imaginatively puts you, it will surely not put you in the classroom of a twenty-first-century American college. Accordingly, the colloquialisms and familiarities of today's college life are out of place. Never open your speech with a salutation like "Hi guys" when something like "Fellow citizens!" would be more appropriate.

Never be friendless when standing at the podium. Do your best to have at least one supporter second your proposal, come to your defense, or admonish inattentive members of the body. Note passing and side conversations, while common occurrences, will likely spoil the effect of your speech; so you and your supporters should insist on order before such behavior becomes too disruptive. Ask the presiding officer to assist you, if necessary, and the Gamemaster as a last resort.

Strategizing. Communication among students is an essential feature of Reacting games. You will find yourself writing emails, texting, attending out-of-class meetings, or gathering for meals on a fairly regular basis. The purpose of frequent communication is to lay out a strategy for advancing your agenda and thwarting the agenda of your opponents and to hatch plots to ensnare individuals troubling to your cause. When communicating with a fellow student in or out of class, always assume that he or she is speaking to you in role. If you want to talk about the "real world," make that clear.

PART 2: HISTORICAL BACKGROUND

CHRONOLOGY

1737 **The Walking Purchase,** or **Ye Running Walk,** cedes territory to Pennsylvania

1742 **Council in Philadelphia** attended by the Iroquois League, Delaware, Shawnee, and Conestoga

- Canassatego, an Iroquois representative, asserts Iroquois hegemony

1744 **March** **King George's War** begins when Britain declares war on France and enters what Europeans call the War of Austrian Succession

June–July **Treaty of Lancaster** results in the Iroquois relinquishing their land claims in Maryland and Virginia

- Subsequently, Virginia expansionists define their colony's borders quite broadly
- Meanwhile, the Shawnee, Delaware, and Mingo populations in the Ohio country continue to grow due to westward migration

1747 **Ohio Company of Virginia** created by Virginia land speculators

1748 **King George's War ends**; Britain and France conclude peace at the Treaty of Aix-la-Chapelle, but everyone continues jockeying for position, especially in the Ohio Country

1752 **Council at Logstown** results in secret confirmation of the 1744 Treaty of Lancaster by some of the Iroquois living in the Ohio Country

- Meanwhile, the Delaware and Shawnee begin negotiating directly with Pennsylvania in defiance of the Iroquois League

1753 **Treaty of Carlisle** between Pennsylvania and several groups of Ohio Indians

1754 **June–July** **Albany Conference** includes the Iroquois League and seven English colonies, including Pennsylvania

- While attending the conference, Pennsylvania agent Conrad Weiser makes deal with "some greedy fellows for money" and purchases a vast tract of land for Pennsylvania that overlaps some of the area claimed by Virginia by way of the Treaty of Lancaster

July **Fort Necessity** surrendered to the French by George Washington after he probed the Ohio Country with Virginia and South Carolina militia

1755 **July** **Braddock's defeat** results from British General Edward Braddock's rash advances toward Fort Duquesne; he and much of his army are killed by French troops and their Indian allies

- Indian raids on frontier farms in Pennsylvania begin soon thereafter

November **Military appropriations made by the Pennsylvania Assembly** include £55,000 for the defense of Pennsylvania; the Penns contribute £5,000

- The assembly also passes legislation raising a volunteer militia and authorizing the construction and garrisoning of a chain of defensive frontier forts; Quaker members largely acquiesce

December **Teedyuscung's Raid** strikes several farms in the Delaware River valley

1756 **April** **Scalp bounties** set by Lieutenant Governor Morris; Quakers protest

May **French and Indian War officially begins** when Britain declares war on France (Europeans will eventually call it the Seven Years' War)

June **Fort Augusta** built at Shamokin with Iroquois permission

July **First Treaty at Easton** attended by Teedyuscung, who becomes "agent and counsel" of Pennsylvania

- **Friendly Association for Regaining and Preserving Peace with the Indians by Pacific Measures** is created by the Quakers

August **William Denny, the new lieutenant governor** of Pennsylvania arrives in Philadelphia

- **Fort Oswego**, the British stronghold on Lake Ontario, falls to the French

September **Kittanning,** an Indian settlement, is successfully attacked by the Pennsylvania militia

- **Lord Loudoun,** commander of imperial forces in North America, orders Pennsylvania to cease independent diplomatic contacts with Indians

October **Benjamin Franklin** becomes the *de facto* leader of anti-Proprietary faction after most Quakers resign from the assembly

November **Second Treaty at Easton** includes Pennsylvania officials, interested Quakers, Iroquois observers, and Indians led by Teedyuscung

THE FOUNDATIONS OF FOREST DIPLOMACY

By the mid-eighteenth century, the area that is now the state of Pennsylvania was home to a variety of intermingled native peoples as well as a burgeoning British colony with an extremely diverse population. The resulting patchwork of authority meant that no one group had a monopoly on power. Instead, the different groups interacted with one another in a shifting network of alliances, coalitions, and antagonisms. Three of these groups—the Iroquois, the Delaware, and the Quakers—laid down the foundation of forest diplomacy in the late seventeenth and early eighteenth centuries, but each of these groups faced serious internal divisions.

When naming indigenous peoples, I generally use the terms *Iroquois League* and *Delaware* when referring to the Haudenosaunee and Lenâpé. This is because these terms are used in scholarly works about the period and also in surviving documents. When referring to both peoples, or other collections of native peoples, I generally use the term *Indians* for the same reason. When referring to European settlers, I generally use the term *Pennsylvanians,* but not in every case.

The Iroquois League

The six nations of the Iroquois League (or Haudenosaunee) are bound together by the story "The Great Law of the Iroquois," which describes the successful efforts of two heroes to cure an evil and misshapen sorcerer. The story explains how the men restored the sorcerer's humanity with a new and powerful set of ceremonies, which included special songs, the presentation of wampum, and a commitment to peace and goodwill. (A version of this story is found on p. 136.)

Before the creation of the Iroquois Confederation, its five founding peoples were trapped in a cycle of violence. Young men sought to prove their prowess by launching raids on neighboring peoples. The families of those killed in these raids called for retaliation, which brought a new round of violence.

The development of these rituals provided an alternative. Instead of pursuing vengeance, grieving families received gifts and formal condolences from the perpetrators of violence. If performed properly and with clear mindedness, the rituals described by the Great Law dissolved anger and hatred. Bereaved families could cope with the loss of relatives without resorting to war. The resulting peace created a powerful confederation; each people retained autonomy, but they attempted to coordinate their actions through the Grand Council, which met at Onondaga.

The Iroquois refer to themselves as the **Haudenosaunee** (pronounced hoe-den-oh-sho-nee), the "People of the Longhouse."

Once they became somewhat coordinated by the Grand Council, the nations of the Iroquois League began to fight wars with their neighbors instead of with one another. In the sixteenth century, they greatly expanded their power and influence in the eastern woodlands of North America by taking captives from other peoples and bringing more of the fur trade with the Europeans under their control. As

Iroquois power grew, the reach of their sophisticated system of diplomacy also expanded. By the time Europeans began settling along the Atlantic coast in the seventeenth century, the rituals of the Great Law established a set of protocols that became the basis for diplomacy between many peoples of the eastern woodlands. For an example of early interactions between Europeans and Indians using these protocols, see Heckwelder's "Coming of Miquon" on p. 102.

Some Indians attempted to use these protocols when they began interacting with European traders and settlers. Many Europeans never attempted to understand these efforts at drawing them in to the clear-minded search for mutual understanding as described in the Great Law, but some recognized the usefulness of the rituals. As the Iroquois became an important pivot in the imperial competition between Britain and France, colonial leaders increasingly saw that their efforts to influence Indians often depended on the proper use of these diplomatic forms.

By the late seventeenth century, trade, warfare, diplomacy, and missionary activity enmeshed the Iroquois in European conflicts, and in 1677 New York became the first colony to forge a "covenant chain" (a mutually beneficial alliance) with the Iroquois. The chain was kept bright with gifts, trade, frequent consultations, and a measure of strategic coordination. This seemed to be a good thing for the Iroquois. This alliance allowed them to establish their **political hegemony** over neighboring peoples, but it became a liability in the late seventeenth century when it pulled them into a disastrous series of wars with France and its Indian allies that lasted until the early eighteenth century.

Political hegemony refers to the preponderant influence of one political entity over another.

At the beginning of the eighteenth century, greatly weakened by these wars, the Iroquois proclaimed their neutrality. This, combined with their influence over trade in firearms, allowed them to seize the diplomatic initiative for half a century and strengthen their influence over neighboring peoples, like the Delaware and Shawnee, who lived to their south. Controlling these peoples provided a barrier against Cherokee and Catawba raiders who struck northward from the far south. In addition, the land inhabited by the Delaware and Shawnee was coveted by the rapidly growing colony of Pennsylvania, which provided the Iroquois with a valuable bargaining chip.

The Delaware

When they first encountered Europeans, the **Lenâpé** lived in small, nearly autonomous communities in the lower Delaware River valley (see map, p. vii). They shared a common language and some cultural practices, but they were not a cohesive "nation." This became problematic when European settlers, the Swedes and the Dutch, first arrived in their

The Delaware call themselves the **Lenâpé** (pronounced len-ah-pay), the "Original People."

section of the Atlantic coast in the mid-seventeenth century. Interested in trade and land, the settlers wanted to open negotiations with the "leaders" of the Lenâpé. Consequently, myriad headmen from various kin groups and villages claimed the right to speak on the behalf of different Lenâpé communities.

Soon after colonists signed a land deal with one of these "kings," another would appear, demanding payment for the same piece of land. This seemed appropriate to the Lenâpé because they, like other eastern woodland Indians, customarily allowed overlapping usage, or **usufruct** rights, over a single piece of territory. Anyone who possessed these rights could use the land for hunting, fishing, and gathering. Because each headman represented a group that possessed such rights, each felt entitled to payment. The Swedes and the Dutch found this infuriating, but given their relative weakness, most saw no alternative to making multiple payments for the same parcel of land.

Usufruct rights allow someone to utilize the resources on a piece of land without owning the land outright.

In the early eighteenth century, epidemics, warfare, and growing pressure from European settlers pushed the Lenâpé northward, farther up the Delaware River valley and westward to the Susquehanna River valley. There they built new villages with other refugees from the east like the Munsee and Mahican. Buffeted by war and disease, they together formed a new group, which came to be known as the "Delaware." Other refugees settled with them. Nanticoke, Conoy, Tutelo, Saponi, Tuscarora, and Shawnee came from the south, and Algonquian speakers came from communities in New England that had been shattered by disease and conflict with the expansionist Puritans. The Delaware were a composite people, and this new label was as much a result of European desires to order their understanding of the complex politics of the frontier as the political realities within these communities.

Regardless of the particulars of the composition of Delaware communities, the Iroquois League claimed hegemony over all of them because much of the land they settled on was once occupied by the **Susquehannock**, a people who had been soundly defeated—and largely forcibly adopted—by the Iroquois in the mid-seventeenth century. As a result, the Iroquois laid claim to Delaware lands with a rationale that Europeans understood: the right of conquest.

Susquehannock returned to the Susquehanna River valley in the early eighteenth century and became known as the Conestoga.

The Quakers

Born of the radicalism of the English Civil War (1642–51), the Quakers, or the Society of Friends, began as a British religious group that rejected most of the conventions of the Church of England, including the sacraments and the priesthood. They believed that there was no authority more ultimate than the "inner light" of the spirit that every individual possessed. In following this inner light, they broke with most Christian traditions of the seventeenth century. Instead of employing

Quaker meetings are religious services that vary in structure; all reflect the Quaker idea everyone possesses an inner light.

clergy to lead their services, members of a **Quaker meeting** simply rose and spoke when the spirit moved them. If the spirit moved women, they too were free to speak. Disregarding hierarchical titles, Quakers called everyone *thee* or *thou*, and in a similarly egalitarian vein, they refused to take oaths and would not remove their hats unless in the presence of God. Disdainful of luxury, they wore plain and unadorned clothing. This commitment to austerity, individualism, and equality horrified most of their countrymen.

The individual relationship with God that lay at the heart of Quakerism could have splintered the movement, but as they matured into an established sect in the late seventeenth century, Quaker meetings began disowning members who did not follow the "spirit of the meeting." This ensured a measure of cohesion and bound the community more tightly together. Quaker leaders also began publishing epistles and pamphlets to promote certain ideas. Prominent among these was the "peaceable testimony," which set forth a commitment to Christian pacifism. This related to one of the issues that galvanized the early movement: paying taxes to fund the military during the English Civil War. As pacifists, many devout Quakers insisted that it would be sinful to financially support state-sanctioned violence. Others walked a more pragmatic path: they refused to directly participate in military action, but they still obediently paid their taxes to the authorities. Despite occasional political compromises of this nature, Quakers were still discriminated against by members of the Church of England.

In 1682, when prominent Quaker William Penn (1644–1718) secured a charter from King Charles II to create the colony of Pennsylvania on the eastern coast of North America, many Quakers chose to leave England. The charter recognized Penn as the sole proprietor of the new colony, which meant that, as far as the Crown was concerned, all the land within the bounds of the colony was his.

Penn sought to supplement this claim by securing title to the land from the different native groups he encountered. In this, he generally followed the precedent set by the Swedish and Dutch settlers who had arrived in the area several decades before him. When their settlements were absorbed into Pennsylvania, Penn continued their practice of purchasing title to the land from local Lenâpé headmen.

Fee simple refers to the permanent and absolute ownership of land with freedom to sell it at will.

Even though Penn tried to be an honest dealer, his efforts to secure exclusive **"fee simple"** title to these lands, rather than traditional usufruct rights, challenged Indian notions about the proper relationship between people and the land. Regardless, he intended the expansion of the colony to be a peaceful and orderly process, so as the proprietor of Pennsylvania he reserved the exclusive right to acquire new Indian lands. Once he had secured title to a particular tract, he began selling and renting it out to European settlers. (On the maps in this game book, areas acquired through these early multiple purchases by Penn are included in the area labeled "uncontested"; see p. vi).

Benefiting from a half century of good relations between Lenâpé and the Swedes and Dutch that preceded him, Penn worked hard to make the new colony a peaceful one. Quaker pacifism pervaded Pennsylvania's policies. Unlike the other colonies of British North America, Pennsylvania did not rely on armed force to expand its territories. Indeed, it did not even organize a militia or construct fortifications. Penn and his fellow Quakers argued that the shoals of the Delaware River provided protection against attack by competing European powers while conciliation and fair treatment preserved the peace with neighboring Indians. If Pennsylvania were to expand, it would do so peaceably.

GROWTH OF PENNSYLVANIA

In the early eighteenth century, Pennsylvania became an attractive destination for European settlers. The availability of land, a peaceful frontier, and a deserved reputation for religious tolerance resulted in a rapidly increasing population. Quakers remained dominant politically, but they were joined by many others, including various German dissenters and Scots-Irish Presbyterians. Immigrants also came from England, and increasingly, these newcomers were Anglican rather than Quaker. Mostly farmers, they pushed the boundaries of white settlement westward. Many purchased newly acquired Indian land from the Proprietors, while others rented farms from the Penns. Some pushed the frontier even farther and squatted on land without much attention to questions of legal ownership.

Although Quakers were renowned for religious toleration, they clearly expected to maintain their dominance of Pennsylvania's legal, social, and cultural life. They largely did so by controlling the elected assembly. Anglicans and Presbyterians often chafed under Quaker rule, but they usually benefited from the colony's prosperity and stability, so they tended to support the Quaker hold on power. As Quakers became a minority, they maintained their political dominance by appealing to various immigrant groups, particularly the Germans, as honest brokers dedicated to maintaining religious freedom.

Challenges to Quaker rule often questioned their commitment to pacifism. Tensions with France and Spain encouraged many to call for the establishment of a militia, but the Pennsylvania Assembly refused. When, under pressure, the assembly made appropriations under the vague rubric "for the Queen's use," Quakers still insisted on appointing a committee to ensure the funds were spent in accordance with their peaceable testimony. As a result, the opponents of the Quakers began arguing that the Quaker determination to practice the tenets of their beliefs made them unfit to govern.

The successes of these policies meant that in the mid-eighteenth century, William Penn's proprietorship was remembered as a golden age of peace and understanding. Subsequent governors of Pennsylvania carefully burnished the image of William Penn peacefully negotiating with the Lenâpé alongside the Delaware River. Yet, while Pennsylvania's Indian policy was unique in form, it was not in effect. The influx of settlers meant that Indian peoples were displaced; the growing European population began moving inland. As more settlers arrived, it became clear that they were there not just to stay, but to transform the landscape to fit their sensibilities. They rapidly cleared trees, introduced livestock, laid out fields for single crops, planted orchards, erected fences and walls, and depleted what remained of the game. Land had become a commodity that could be owned and exploited.

The Covenant Chain

The Indian policies of William Penn had an abiding legacy, and until the middle of the eighteenth century, Pennsylvanians enjoyed relative peace. They sustained this tranquility with a flourishing fur trade and generous gifts intended to brighten Pennsylvania's "covenant chain" with the Iroquois League and their tributaries. This relationship helped the Iroquois develop into a major powerbroker, but this was offset by their mounting problems with famine, disease, alcoholism, and out-migration to the west.

As their power ebbed, they found it increasingly difficult to exert control over neighboring peoples like the Delaware and Shawnee, particularly as large numbers of these peoples left the Susquehanna River valley and migrated farther west across the Allegheny Mountains. The lands of the Ohio Country lay beyond the reach of Iroquois power.

After the forging of the covenant chain, the Iroquois referred to the **Proprietary** of Pennsylvania as "Brother Onas." This signified their equality.

In an attempt to shore up the dwindling power of their league, a group of Iroquois leaders began to align more closely with the growing power of Pennsylvania. In the 1730s, the chief negotiator for the proprietors of Pennsylvania, Conrad Weiser, helped broker an agreement: if Pennsylvania suspended independent diplomatic relations with the Delaware, Shawnee, and other smaller Indian peoples, the Iroquois would maintain order on the frontier. When dealing with Pennsylvania, the diverse interests of these peoples would now be represented by their "uncles," the Iroquois. If the Iroquois agreed to speak for all of the Indians in the area *and* they asserted right of ownership over vast tracts of land due to their conquest of the Susquehannock, then they became (in European eyes) a singular authority from which Pennsylvania could purchase clear title in fee simple. This arrangement greatly simplified the expansion of Pennsylvania's land claims. The Iroquois benefited by collecting large payments for land over which (in Indian eyes) they possessed only tenuous authority.

The rapidly growing population of Pennsylvania made the colony ready to buy land, even if Iroquois rights were questionable. This arrangement was particularly attractive to John, Richard, and Thomas Penn—William Penn's sons, who had inherited the charter to become the proprietors of the colony in 1718. They jettisoned both their father's faith and his tradition of fair dealing with the Indians. They were interested in Pennsylvania for one reason only: profit. Consequently, in 1736, the grasping, avaricious, and Anglican Thomas Penn (1702–1775), arranged the purchase of much of the Susquehanna River valley from the Iroquois rather than the Indians who actually lived there. (On the maps, the area purchased by Thomas Penn is also included in the area labeled "uncontested"; see p. vi).

In the eyes of Penn's sons, this land was already theirs because in 1701 their father had purchased the area from the Conestoga. The Conestoga had happily sold the lands, which they could claim by right of occupation but which they lacked the ability to hold against the power of the Iroquois. This meant that Penn's sons saw their willingness to purchase these lands as particularly generous, but many Indians probably viewed the purchase with skepticism. In the hands of his sons, the system that William Penn created to ensure the peaceful expansion of Pennsylvania had started to break down.

Walking Purchase of 1737

The alliance between Pennsylvania's proprietors and the Iroquois resulted in another deal in 1737. Eager to expand their holdings, Penn's sons arranged a devious land cession by which Pennsylvania acquired from the Delaware a large block of territory on the western bank of the Delaware River. Many angry Delawares refused to recognize this blatantly crooked land grab, which they called "ye Running Walk."

It began when two of Penn's sons produced what they claimed was a 1700 treaty between their father and a group of Delawares that entitled them to a plot of land stretching as far north as a man could walk in a day and a half, following the river. Pressured by the Iroquois, Delaware leaders verified the legitimacy of the treaty. The Penns subsequently hired runners to make the "walk" along cleared pathways, which allowed them to cover sixty miles. They ignored the stipulation to follow the course of the river, and instead struck inland, which further expanded the tract. This gave Pennsylvania claim to all the territory between the Delaware and Lehigh rivers, much of which was occupied by the Delaware in what was known as the Walking Purchase (see map on p. vi).[1]

Although Delaware protests to this absurd interpretation were legitimate, Penn's sons considered them immaterial because they had decided the Delaware people were subordinate to the Iroquois League. As far as they were concerned, any dispute about the Walking Purchase was resolved in 1742 at a treaty council

---

1. William A. Starna, "The Diplomatic Career of Canasatego," in *Friends and Enemies in Penn's Woods: Indians, Colonists, and the Racial Construction of Pennsylvania*, William A. Pencak and Daniel K. Richter, eds. (University Park: Pennsylvania State University Press, 2004), p. 149.

in Philadelphia attended by representatives of the Iroquois, Delaware, Shawnee, and Conestoga. After Pennsylvania's lieutenant governor (a loyal employee of the Penns) plied the Iroquois representative, Canassatego, with gifts, he returned the favor by supporting the Walking Purchase, severely chastising the Delaware for bringing it up, assigning them the status of women, and forbidding them from involving themselves in future land deals. (See "Delaware as Women" on p. 151.) He insisted that their Iroquois "uncles" would speak for them henceforth. This perfectly aligned with the interests of Penn's sons. (Excerpts from the 1742 treaty are on p. 67.)

After this, although some Delaware, particularly those who had been converted to Christianity, remained in the Delaware River valley, most of them subsequently relocated to the Susquehanna River's north branch, settling in the Wyoming Valley alongside Shawnee who had been there for several decades. Some moved even farther west, crossing the Allegheny Mountains, and settling in the Ohio Country. These events bolstered the confidence of Penn's sons in the power of the Iroquois, even as it was slipping away.

King George's War and the Treaty of Lancaster

In March 1744, the two great imperial rivals in North America renewed hostilities when Britain once again declared war on France, beginning what Europeans called the War of Austrian Succession and what many in the colonies referred to as King George's War. In some ways, this conflict aided the Iroquois. Occupying a pivotal position between New France and British North America, they attempted to play the imperial ambitions of the great powers and growing colonial land hunger to their advantage. In the short term they succeeded, but by agreeing to the terms of the Treaty of Lancaster in 1744, they inadvertently put forces into motion that would eventually result in war and their decline in power.

In the summer of 1744, representatives from the Iroquois League and the colonies of Pennsylvania, Maryland, and Virginia met together for a grand treaty conference in Lancaster, Pennsylvania. In the course of these negotiations, the Iroquois relinquished their rather tenuous land claims on the frontiers of Maryland and Virginia in exchange for gifts. This initially appeared to be a good deal for the Iroquois, for they had, in essence, gotten paid for lands that they never actually controlled. However, the stunningly expansive definition of "Virginia" that appeared in that colony's charter encouraged many Virginians to assert their subsequent land claims quite broadly. (Extensive excerpts of the Treaty of Lancaster appear on p. 70.)

Following the Treaty of Lancaster, Virginia claimed the entire Ohio River valley and a gigantic slab of North America that extended all the way to the Pacific Ocean. Few outside of

Indians referred to Virginia as **Assaragoa** and Maryland as **Tocarry-hogan.**

Virginia considered these claims legitimate, but that did not prevent Virginia land speculators from creating the Ohio Company of Virginia in 1747. Despite their conspicuous lack of success, their efforts to erect a settlement in Ohio angered the French; most of the Indians living in the Ohio River valley; and William Penn's sons, the proprietors of Pennsylvania.

Although much of the conflict in North America ended in 1744, the war in Europe continued for another four years. Britain and France concluded peace at the Treaty of Aix-la-Chapelle in 1748, but continuing tensions ensured that it was little more than a cease-fire. The following year, Pennsylvania extended its land claims to the west by gaining title to more Indian land. In an increasingly familiar process, it began when the proprietors of Pennsylvania made what appeared to be a small purchase from the Iroquois. They then defined it as encompassing most of the remaining Indian land east of the Susquehanna River. Again, both the proprietors and the Iroquois benefited. The proprietors received what they considered to be legitimate legal ownership of a large piece of territory while the Iroquois got wagonloads of gifts in exchange for lands over which they had little actual control. (On the map, this area is included in the area labeled "uncontested"; see p. vi).

The Ohio Valley and Fort Duquesne

In the early 1750s, the fertile Ohio River valley continued to be a flashpoint for imperial ambition. Predominantly populated by Shawnee and Delaware who had fled European settlement and Iroquois hegemony on the eastern side of the mountains, it was also home to smaller groups of Indian refugees from the east and several western tribes. Further complicating things was the presence of Iroquois immigrants on the southern shore of Lake Erie. The Grand Council of the Iroquois League in Onondaga possessed only tenuous control over this group, known to the English as the **Mingo**. The upper Ohio Valley made a good home for these disparate groups, often collectively referred to as the "Ohio Indians," but as historian Francis Jennings observes, "Their land was too rich and beautiful, and too strategically located, for them to be left alone by powers stronger than themselves."[2]

The **Mingo** were Iroquois migrants to the Ohio Country who did not recognize the authority of the Grand Council in Onondaga. Most of them lived along the eastern shore of Lake Erie.

Europeans came at the Ohio Valley from several different directions. First, the Virginians began negotiating with several groups of Ohio Indians in an effort to confirm their expansive interpretation of the 1744 Treaty of Lancaster. Then Pennsylvania began negotiating directly with the Delaware and Shawnee in an effort to head off the Virginians. Proprietary agent **Conrad Weiser** reasoned that if the Iroquois could not counter the threat,

Indians named **Conrad Weiser** *Tarachawagon* or "You Must Hold Up the Sky for Us."

2. Francis Jennings, *Empires of Fortune: Crowns, Colonies & Tribes in the Seven Years War in America* (New York: Norton, 1988), pp. 19–20.

TIP

The Delaware made an ancestral claim to much of the Ohio Country. For an articulation of this claim, see Zeisberger's "Delawares and the Allegheny River Valley" on p. 107.

Pennsylvania must act alone. In a repudiation of their partnership with the Iroquois League, Pennsylvania went so far as to recognize Shingas, a Delaware headman, as a "king" in 1751. Some Iroquois on the scene attempted to save face by appointing Shingas as king, but it was clear that the covenant chain between Pennsylvania and the Iroquois was becoming uncoupled. If the Iroquois could no longer aid Pennsylvania's ambitions, Weiser and his employers appeared ready to let the partnership end.

A third group of ambitious imperialists came into the Ohio Country from New France. Laying claim to the area by right of discovery, the French saw the Ohio Country as an essential component of their strategy of encirclement: if they could hold the area it would provide a critical link between their tenuous posts along the Mississippi River and their more fully developed colony in Canada. Together, these holdings would contain British North America to the eastern fringes of the continent, allowing French influence and trade to dominate the vast interior. Often operating in concert with Indian allies from the Great Lakes region, the French began building forts down the west face of the Allegheny Mountains, attacking pro-British Indians, and driving British traders out of the villages of the Ohio Indians.

In an effort to gauge British reaction to the incursions of the French, several delegations of Ohio Indians traveled across the Allegheny Mountains to Virginia and Pennsylvania. One of the resulting negotiations occurred at Carlisle in 1753. (Excerpts of the 1753 treaty appear on p. 92.) It did little to convince the Indians that Pennsylvania was willing or able to take action to counter the French advance into the Ohio Country. Consequently, the Ohio Indians stood by when, in April 1754, a strong French force seized a far-flung Virginia outpost at the strategically significant forks of the Ohio. They subsequently erected a solid, European-style fortification, Fort Duquesne (pronounced DU-kane), to dominate this important strategic location. This marked the shift of initiative to the French.

The combination of these events meant that by the mid-1750s, imperial ambitions had strained relations between Pennsylvanians and their Indian neighbors to the breaking point. Most Ohio Indians accepted French influence radiating southward from Canada. This placed the Delaware and Shawnee who remained in the Susquehanna River valley, which lay to the east of the Allegheny Mountains, in a very difficult position. They were boxed in between the advancing settlers of Pennsylvania and Virginia, the rising influence of the French in the Ohio Country, and their erstwhile Iroquois "uncles" to the north. These problems were exacerbated by the deepening relationship between the western branches of their peoples and the French.

The Albany Conference and Washington's Defeat

In the summer of 1754 representatives from the Iroquois League and seven English colonies, including Pennsylvania, met in Albany, New York, in an attempt to renew the covenant chain with the Iroquois and to discuss possible responses to the growing French presence in the Ohio Valley. The meeting was overseen by the Crown-appointed superintendent of Indian affairs, William Johnson.

Best known for the unrealized "Plan of Union" proposed by Pennsylvania representative Benjamin Franklin, the Albany Conference was otherwise unremarkable, except for a series of land deals that were hatched **"in the bushes"**—away from the formal proceedings. In one important instance, Pennsylvania's chief negotiator, Conrad Weiser, used his mastery of forest diplomacy, liquor, and well-placed gifts to forge a deal with some important Iroquois; he purchased a vast tract of land for Pennsylvania, which overlapped the area claimed by Virginia by way of the Treaty of Lancaster. This land was, not incidentally, occupied primarily by the Delaware, Shawnee, and Mingo.

Negotiations **in the bushes** were often important for frontier diplomacy. Away from the formal protocols of the treaty council, these talks, which were often accompanied by the free flow of liquor, were often where important deals were hatched.

In some ways this marked a return to the old partnership between Pennsylvania and the Iroquois. Pennsylvania was once again purchasing land through the Iroquois—land the Iroquois did not really control. (On the maps this area is included in the area labeled "1754"; see p. vi.) But this purchase was built on even shakier ground than earlier deals because it had been made without the approval of the Grand Council in Onondaga. Consequently, many believed this deal was void, but it was considered bona fide by the proprietors.[3]

While the Albany Conference was still in session, the participants heard word of the sharp defeat suffered by a rash group of Virginians led into the Ohio Country by George Washington. Their goal was to assert Virginia's claims by taking Fort Duquesne, but the group was unable to get substantial aid from local Indians through their Iroquois intermediaries. Having gravely underestimated the power of the French and their Indian allies, Washington's force of Virginia militia was outmatched and forced to surrender at Great Meadows on July 4, 1754. The tenuous peace between France and Britain was unraveling. War was coming again.

---

3. Francis Jennings, "Iroquois Alliances in American History," in *The History and Culture of Iroquois Diplomacy: An Interdisciplinary Guide to the Treaties of the Six Nations and Their League*, Francis Jennings, ed. (Syracuse, NY: Syracuse University Press, 1985), p. 52.

WAR IN THE BORDERLANDS

In response to the French victory against Washington's failed incursion into the Ohio Country, London dispatched General Edward Braddock and a force of British regulars to put things right in North America. Charged with organizing several simultaneous offensives against New France, Braddock himself led a strong force toward Fort Duquesne in 1755. His deliberate march westward across the Alleghenies was hampered by rough and unfamiliar terrain, a lengthy supply train, and an almost total lack of Indian guides. Disdainful of Indian auxiliaries, Braddock alienated most of the Indians who offered their services by promising that victory over the French would be followed by English settlement of the Ohio Country. After a long march, Braddock's force was attacked by the French and their Indian allies as it neared the fort. British regulars fought with great determination, but their tactics were poorly suited to forest warfare. Consequently, they were slaughtered. Most of the colonial troops, including those led by George Washington, fled. Mortally wounded, Braddock died on the retreat to Pennsylvania.

Most of the Indians who accompanied the French in this attack were their old allies from the Great Lakes, but a few Mingo, Delaware, and Shawnee joined in. After Braddock's defeat more and more of these Ohio Indians defied the Iroquois and took up the hatchet against the British. This led to the beginning of a series of destructive and terrifying raids on settlements along the Pennsylvania, Maryland, and Virginia frontier. Settlers fled the once-peaceful Susquehanna Valley for shelter in the towns to the east. At first the Indians who lived in the Susquehanna Valley stayed on the sidelines, caught, as historian Francis Jennings puts it, "between the Iroquois hammer and Pennsylvania's anvil."[4]

Some Indian leaders in this area even hoped for financing and supplies from Pennsylvania so they could make war on the French. Hamstrung by the uncooperative Quaker-dominated assembly that refused to make war appropriations, Pennsylvania's proprietary-appointed lieutenant governor could not offer arms or support to them. Instead, he simply directed them to obey the instructions of their would-be hegemons, the Iroquois.

During the fall of 1755 and the winter that followed more Shawnee and Delaware joined the war against the British. Some had been threatened by ardent pro-war Indians—the so-called war party. Others were encouraged by French promises of weapons and supplies. Still others joined in search of revenge for decades of abuse by avaricious Pennsylvanians with their plows, diseases, liquor, and unscrupulous traders. Finally, but not inconsequentially, some young men simply relished the opportunity for war. Combat brought manhood and, to the skilled and lucky, captives.

4. Jennings, "Iroquois Alliances in American History," pp. 53–54.

By spring hundreds of Pennsylvania settlers had been killed. Hundreds more had been taken captive. (It was probably not coincidental that the wife, son, and daughter of the one man who finished the entire arduous "walk" of 1737 were among the dead.) While many of these captives were adopted or ritually sacrificed, some were sold to the French, who then transported them to their settlements in Canada. Some of these prisoners were ransomed, but most remained under French control. Regardless of their intended use, once they were taken, captives needed to be fit enough to keep up with a forced march through the forest. This meant that healthy and unwounded prisoners were usually taken while elderly, ill, or injured captives were executed. This provided scalps. While these were not as valuable as living captives, they still offered evidence of a warrior's prowess. (The account of John Cox, a Pennsylvanian taken captive in the resulting raids, appears on p. 133.) For more on raids along the frontier, see "Teedyuscung's Raid" on p. 154.

TIP

In the Coda at the end of the game, the commissioners of the assembly may make appropriations for a variety of purposes.

Panic and Appropriations

Panicked and vengeful white refugees from the frontier soon filled Pennsylvania's towns. Largely Germans and Scots-Irish immigrants, they heaped scorn upon the inaction of Pennsylvania's government. No militia had been raised because of a deadlock between the Quaker-dominated assembly and the lieutenant governor that had begun in 1740. The assembly demanded that new taxes would include a levy on proprietary lands, which had heretofore been tax exempt. The lieutenant governor, an employee of the proprietors, dutifully protected their interests by vetoing the act. In response, the assembly refused to levy taxes on *anyone*.

But pressure from frontier refugees helped break the stalemate in November 1755, with a legislative compromise crafted, in part, by Benjamin Franklin, a leading member of the assembly. The arrangement began with a £5,000 "gift" from the proprietors, which was matched by £55,000 in taxes, which were levied by the assembly and earmarked in a sufficiently vague way: "for the King's use." These funds helped raise a volunteer militia and paid for the construction of a chain of defensive frontier forts, which were intended to obstruct French and Indian raids.

The assembly maintained its authority by insisting that it possessed the exclusive right to grant and control supplies purchased with these funds. As proof, they appointed seven commissioners to oversee their disbursement. Unlike the taxes raised during previous wars, these funds were used for explicitly military purposes because the commissioners included pragmatic defense Quakers and the expansionist Benjamin Franklin.

NOTE

Several **commissioners of the Pennsylvania Assembly,** including Benjamin Franklin, will attend the Treaty Council.

Quaker Idealism

Quakers had sat out earlier wars with some success, but the situation in 1755 was different because war had come to Pennsylvania's previously peaceful frontier. This gave the proprietors a golden opportunity to pry the Quakers out of the assembly. Their pacifism provided a useful fulcrum. King George's War was a distant conflict, but the new struggle was in their backyard. Quakers now found themselves insisting on pursuing a policy of nonviolence toward groups that had carried the war into Pennsylvania: the French and their Indian allies. Furthermore, they did so when the streets of Philadelphia were crowded with angry refugees from groups they relied on for their continued political influence.

Initially, expediency won the day because the Quakers feared that stepping away from power would result in the conversion of the government of Pennsylvania to something more closely resembling the royal colony of Virginia, with its compulsory militia law, established Church of England, and growing reliance on slavery (an institution the Quakers increasingly condemned). Consequently, the Quaker-dominated assembly acquiesced to the funding of various military measures, as long as they remained defensive in character.

Quaker purist John Woolman criticized the pragmatism of the so-called defense Quakers who supported these appropriations and issued epistles encouraging Quakers to leave government if they could not love God and their neighbors. Other purists, like Samuel Fothergill, condemned assemblymen as grasping sinners who had turned against their faith. Another, Anthony Benezet, advised them to obey the teachings of Christ, imitate his example, and "*resist not evil,* but rather suffer wrong and thus overcome evil with good."[5] (Woolman's "Epistle from the Society of Friends" appears on p. 110.)

Together, the purists demanded a revival of sectarian strictness and a retreat from politics. Many Quakers listened and refused to pay their taxes, but most Quaker assemblymen remained unconvinced. They would try to balance their faith with political necessity.

War in Earnest

In April 1756, after prodding by hawkish members of the assembly and consultation with the Iroquois, Lieutenant Governor Robert Hunter Morris declared war on "enemy Indians" and set bounties on their scalps. This was a dramatic departure from Pennsylvania's previously conciliatory attitude, and because of the difficulty

---

5. Sydney V. James, *A People among Peoples: Quaker Benevolence in Eighteenth-Century America* (Cambridge: Harvard University Press, 1963), p. 171. See also, John Woolman, "To Friends on the Continent of America," in *The Journal and Essays of John Woolman,* A. M. Gummere, ed. (New York: Macmillan, 1922), pp. 177–79.

in determining the specific source of any one particular scalp, this policy potentially endangered all Indians. This was war in earnest, and it was increasingly a war between peoples. Everyone was now a potential target. (For details on scalp bounties and other war measures undertaken by Morris, see "Deliberations of the Governor's Council" on p. 122.)

Many Quakers protested Morris's aggressive moves, but the passions of war made their commitment to principle increasingly awkward and unpopular. On one occasion refugees from Gnadenhütten, a settlement that had been attacked and burned by raiders, paraded a corpse-filled wagon through Philadelphia. The wagon was followed by a mob that cursed both the Indians and Quakers. Some Quaker purists saw the war as the wrath of God. After seeing the wagon, Quaker John Churchman wrote:

> The sight of the dead bodies and the outcry of people were very afflicting and shocking to me: Standing at the door at a friend's house as they passed along, my mind was humbled and turned much inward when it was made secretly to cry; *What will become of Pennsylvania?* For it felt to me that many did not consider, that the sins of the inhabitants, pride, profane swearing, drunkenness with other wickedness were the cause, that the Lord had suffered this calamity and scourge to come upon them: the weight of my exercise increasing as I walked along the street; at length it was said in my soul, *This Land is polluted with blood, and in the day of inquisition for blood, it will not only be required at the frontiers and borders, but even in this place where these bodies are now seen.*[6]

Quakers were also threatened by events in London where an Anglican clergyman, William Smith, published *A Brief State of the Province of Pennsylvania*, which leveled a number of serious charges against the Quakers. In essence, the pamphlet accused them of facilitating the French conquest of Pennsylvania. Underwritten by the proprietor Thomas Penn, this pamphlet created a stir in the imperial capital, and some began to discuss requiring Quakers to take a loyalty oath—a requirement that would go against Quaker prohibitions on oath taking. (Excerpts from *A Brief State* appear on p. 112.)

Threatened by the possibility of a loyalty oath, reminded of the traditional Quaker commitment to pacifism by purists, and hounded by accusations of disloyalty and treason, several Quakers, led by James Pemberton, resigned their seats in the assembly in June 1756, but others, including the Assembly Speaker Isaac Norris, remained as defense Quakers.

---

6. John Churchman, *An Account of the Gospel Labours, and Christian Experiences of a Faithful Minister of Christ, John Churchman* (Philadelphia: Joseph Crukshank, 1779), p. 175; quoted in Robert Daiutolo Jr., "The Role of Quakers in Indian Affairs during the French and Indian War," *Quaker History* 77, no. 1 (spring 1988): 6.

The deep disagreements between purists and defense Quakers broke apart the economically and politically powerful Quaker bloc that had dominated Pennsylvania politics since its founding. After the departure of Pemberton, few Quakers remained in the government, but many of those outside the halls of power, like his brother Israel, remained determined to forge a peace. If necessary, they would do this as private citizens. Ironically, in the wake of a long-sought political victory over the Quakers, the proprietors found they now had *two* powerful political challengers instead of one. Franklin and his associates in the assembly demanded the authority to levy taxes, organize the defense of the colony, and prosecute the war, while the Quakers, led by wealthy merchant Israel Pemberton, sought to circumvent proprietary control over diplomacy. Neither had much respect for the authority of the proprietors or the lieutenant governor, who ruled in their absence.

Recent Military Events

In the months after Benjamin Franklin broke the funding deadlock in November 1755, Pennsylvania's new militia remained next to useless. Funds were also spent to construct a chain of forts and blockhouses along the Kittochtinny Hills. They failed to prevent the infiltration of Indian raiders. But some signs of capable resistance began to appear. Foremost was the construction of Fort Augusta, which was built at the forks of the Susquehanna with Iroquois approval in June 1756. Situated beside the ruins of the Indian town of Shamokin (which was burned the previous fall), it represented Pennsylvania's first real attempt to project its developing military power into the Susquehanna Valley. (For details on Pennsylvania's military mobilization, see the "Deliberations of the Governor's Council" on p. 122.)

Despite the new fort, French and Indian raiders continued to strike farms on the frontier with near impunity. A month after the construction of Fort Augusta, a party of French and Delaware attacked and burned Pennsylvania's westernmost military outpost, Fort Granville, on the Juniata River. This marked the beginning of a new string of military defeats for British forces in North America, which included the fall of Fort Oswego, the sole British trading post on the Great Lakes. After the British commander surrendered, many of the Indians accompanying the expedition killed and scalped the sick and wounded, looted the fort, and took captives.

In September 1756, Pennsylvania's military potential began to show when the Pennsylvania militia carried out a moderately successful raid against the Indian settlement at Kittanning on the *western* side of the Alleghenies. The militia suffered heavy casualties and killed indiscriminately, but succeeded in killing Captain Jacobs, the Delaware leader of the attack on Fort Granville. (For details of this raid, see "John Armstrong's Account of the Kittanning Fight" on p. 127.)

In Philadelphia, the withdrawal of the Quaker purists from the assembly significantly shifted the political situation. In October 1756, the annual elections to the Pennsylvania Assembly redrew the map of Pennsylvania politics. Anglicans and Presbyterians, who supported the war effort, filled the seats vacated by the Quakers who resigned the preceding June. This greatly strengthened the hand of Benjamin Franklin as the leader of the anti-proprietary group, and ensured that the leaders of the assembly would play a major role in making wartime decisions.

These political shifts in Philadelphia were followed by additional military reverses in upstate New York, where French regulars and Canadians were joined by the most impressive host of Indian warriors ever gathered by New France. These included traditional French allies like the Ottawa, Abenaki, and Ojibwa as well as warriors from farther west, including the Winnebago, Sauk, Fox, and even a handful of Iowa. News of the victory at Fort Oswego had drawn them eastward, hoping for glory and captives. The French commander, Louis-Joseph de Montcalm, used them to besiege Fort William Henry, which surrendered in August 1757.

Montcalm promised the defenders safe passage to New York, but the Indians would not be denied their plunder, trophies, and captives, so they fell upon the British troops, militiamen, and camp followers as they evacuated the fort. Montcalm wanted to honor his promise and demanded their release, but many of the Indians preferred scalps to nothing, so many killed their captives. The French subsequently arranged for the ransom of many of the surviving captives, but hundreds were lost.

With the fall of Fort William Henry, the initiative seemed to have shifted to the French and their Indian allies, but French power was fragile. It relied on a tenuous supply line across the Atlantic and allies who fought for reasons other than imperial ambition. After two years of war, many Indians were ready to head for home. This made it difficult for the French to build on their victories. In places like Pennsylvania, the French and their allies also faced an increasingly determined enemy. Pennsylvania's frontier, which had been wide open, had become a hard target.

A CHANCE FOR PEACE

As a result of these actions, what began as a local brushfire war expanded into renewed hostilities between Britain and France on a global scale. Ultimately, this would be referred to as the Seven Years' War. Despite the widening conflict, various groups of Pennsylvanians and Indians were determined to broker a local peace on the Pennsylvania frontier. If achieved, such a peace could end fighting between the colony of Pennsylvania and the Delaware, even if the larger conflict between the French, the British, and their various allies continued.

In the United States this conflict is often referred to as the **French and Indian War**. Elsewhere, it is generally known as the **Seven Years' War**, but some historians prefer the "Great War for Empire."

* * *

As the game begins in late 1757, the military situation on the Pennsylvania frontier has stabilized, but the initiative clearly remains with the French and their Indian allies. Raids on farms and counterattacks on Indian settlements have almost completely depopulated the area between the Allegheny Mountains and the Kittochtinny Hills. A few years earlier the Susquehanna Valley was home to thousands of Indian and European settlers. Now occasional parties of Pennsylvania militia and Indian warriors are the only people to be found amid the ruins. Indian towns like Shamokin, multi-ethnic settlements like Gnadenhütten, farms along the Juniata River and Penn's Creek, and the Delaware and Shawnee villages of the Wyoming Valley have all been destroyed.

For the past year or so, Quaker diplomatic efforts orchestrated by Israel Pemberton have been reaching out to members of the Delaware "peace party," which is particularly strong among those who consider the Susquehanna River valley their home. Many of the Delaware currently reside across the mountains in the Ohio Country or farther north with their "uncles," the Iroquois, but they would like to return home to plant crops and rebuild their lives. Many of the men spent their time raiding rather than hunting, so meat, furs, and skins are all in short supply. The failure of the French to provide supplies to offset these hardships pushed a few Indian leaders led by the Delaware war captain Teedyuscung to enter into initial peace talks as early as July 1756.

Israel Pemberton's efforts come under the official auspices of the ponderously named **Friendly Association for Regaining and Preserving Peace with the Indians by Pacific Measures.**

These talks were facilitated by a group of wealthy and influential Quakers led by Israel Pemberton, who some now call the "king of the Quakers." He managed what amounted to an independent foreign policy by entertaining Indian representatives at his home in Philadelphia, coordinating the collection of contributions, and delivering £2,000 in gifts. Subsequently, through persuasion, generosity, and persistence, Pemberton has arranged for the treaty council that is the centerpiece of this game.

Many disapprove of these efforts. Among them are the two most highly placed imperial officials in North America: Lieutenant General John Campbell, earl of Loudoun, who has been acting as the overall military commander of British forces in North America since July 1755, and William Johnson, the superintendent of Indian affairs in Albany, New York. They are both frustrated by Pennsylvania's efforts to broker a separate peace with the Delaware. They think the treaty should be handled by Johnson. In fact, Loudoun recently wrote a letter to Pennsylvania's new lieutenant governor, William Denny, ordering the cessation of the negotiations that are about to begin. Members of the assembly and provincial council, led by Provincial Secretary Richard Peters, prevailed on Denny to ignore this letter. Consequently, Johnson dispatched George Croghan as his personal representative.

Military Forces

By late 1757, a number of different military forces were present in Pennsylvania. The following sections outline their respective strengths and weaknesses.

The French Although they sometimes embed small groups of Canadian militia and French officers in Indian raiding parties, the French do not have significant forces deployed to the region other than their garrison at Fort Duquesne and a chain of smaller posts on the Allegheny River. Fort Duquesne is a capably built European-style fortification that could probably withstand a sustained siege.

Indians Indians are, quite naturally, the past masters of forest warfare. The arrival of Europeans in North America encouraged Indians to develop skills and tactics that made them preeminently capable raiders, scouts, and skirmishers. They have little interest in fighting set-piece battles, so they are not proficient at maintaining sieges or carrying fortifications, but their ability to move quickly through rough country allows them to bypass strongpoints that would need to be taken by a European army to protect its lines of supply.

> **NOTE**
>
> All of the Indian players have some influence over Indian warriors. They can attempt to persuade them to take specific actions during the final game session, the Coda.

One great weakness of Indian fighters is their dependence on firearms. Fighting and hunting require significant amounts of ammunition, which must be procured from whites. By the winter of 1756–57, the Indians fighting against Pennsylvania began running low on ammunition. French forts in the Ohio Country are on the end of a very long supply line, so they are an unreliable source of resupply. Some munitions are seized in raids, but they are insufficient to support a high tempo of operations, especially because Indians still need to hunt. As a consequence, reopening the arms trade is expected to be one of the most contentious issues at the upcoming treaty council.

Even if they possessed it, the French would probably be reluctant to provide Indians with great amounts of ammunition because they know, from experience, that few Indians are interested in the rigors of a long campaign. Instead of hammering away at an opponent's defenses as is expected in European-style war, most Indians are content to return home after a single victory. If scalps or captives are taken, honor is assured. Why fight on?

Pennsylvania Militia The Pennsylvania militia consists of small units of poorly trained volunteers raised for community defense. They are usually equipped with weapons, but they are expected to provide their own clothing and supplies. Although many colonies in British North America have long-standing militias, Pennsylvania did not have one until the Militia Act of 1755 authorized the creation of a volunteer militia.

The militia is essentially for local self-defense, and its units rarely leave the areas in which they were raised. When taken out of their home districts, their lack of discipline leads to chaos, poor sanitation, sickness, desertion, and death. As a result, they are (with a few exceptions) used to garrison the small forts and blockhouses that were built along the frontier in the hopes of interdicting Indian raiders.

> **TIP**
>
> Players interested in launching offensive military actions using the militia should consult "John Armstrong's Account of the Kittanning Fight" on p. 127.

In practice they rarely leave the vicinity of their defensive works, but small units, such as the men led by Colonel John Armstrong at Kittanning, may occasionally be able to mount offensive operations.

Most militia officers are elected by their men. The highest ranking officers are appointed by the assembly, but all officer commissions must be confirmed by the lieutenant governor in his capacity as commander-in-chief of provincial forces.

British Regulars One of the difficulties in using militia for offensive operations is the short term of their enlistment and the readiness with which they desert. This is a stark contrast to British regulars who often serve for "life"—usually about twenty years. Commitment aids discipline and ensures that the men can remain in the field for the duration of a campaign even if it requires months of hard living under canvas.

Regulars are a formidable force as long as they fight something resembling a mid-eighteenth-century European war with its use of artillery and emphasis on taking and holding strategic locations like forts. It's important to note that such efforts take a significant amount of time because they require cumbersome supply and artillery trains. Besieging forts is one of the things regulars do best, but while it would be very difficult for militia to take a post like Fort Duquesne without the assistance of regulars, it would not be impossible.

While regulars bring devastating musketry and artillery to bear in battle, they often have difficulty when fighting irregulars in rough country like hills and forests, which abound in the eastern woodlands of North America. When fighting in the Indian manner, their determination to hold formation and their brilliant uniforms can become liabilities rather than strengths. This weakness was dramatically illustrated by Braddock's defeat near Fort Duquesne in 1755.

The second major drawback to using regulars in the colonies is their lack of respect for the locals. When Braddock's troops were in Pennsylvania in 1755 they plundered the inhabitants; insulted, abused, and imprisoned those who complained; looked down on officers of the militia; and generally exasperated the populace. While the militia often melts back into the community for bed and board, regulars need barracks and supplies. When these are absent, the men rely on quartering in the community. The prospect of quartering regular troops in private homes is a horrifying one for many Pennsylvanians. The officers are often arrogant and demanding, and the men, drawn from the lowest orders of British society and hardened by war, are often coarse and foul brutes.

Royal American Regiment After Braddock's defeat in 1755, the need for scouts and skirmishers became abundantly clear. Unfortunately, proficient backwoods fighters (other than Indians) are often unreliable and are usually not available in large numbers. Consequently, Parliament recently authorized the creation of a special "Royal American" regiment intended for forest warfare in the colonies. It is intended to blend the discipline and reliability of regulars with the speed and maneuverability of the militia.

At this point, it is a disappointment. Few frontiersmen have enlisted—they balk at the discipline. Instead, these regiments are largely composed of desperate, unruly Germans and Irish. These units are understrength, badly equipped, and indifferently led. The Pennsylvania Assembly has refused to appropriate any money for their benefit, so there are no large formations of British regulars in Pennsylvania at the present, but one of the game players, the British Major, is attempting to raise one. If the assembly appropriates funds for the Royal Americans during the Coda, the British Major shall command them.

PART 3: THE GAME

MAJOR ISSUES FOR DEBATE

Everyone should pay close attention to the speeches presented by other players, but to understand the ideas that lie behind them, everyone must study the documents. Certain documents shed light on particular issues. The following will be the main topics for discussion during the game.

Diplomacy

The vast majority of participants in the Treaty Council are interested in restoring peace to the frontier, but there is a great deal of disagreement about the terms of such a peace. There is also disagreement about the proper form of a peace agreement.

Gifts Reciprocal gift giving is central to the spirit of forest diplomacy. Indians expect gifts. Who will give them? When will they be delivered? What sort of gifts will there be?

> The Treaty of Lancaster illustrates the possibility of trading gifts for land (p. 70).
>
> The Carlisle Treaty illustrates Pennsylvania's recent unwillingness to deliver gifts that have been promised (p. 92).

Peace Few seek peace at any cost, so everyone must weigh the benefits of war and peace. How are they balanced in this specific case?

> Woolman's epistle provides a pacifist critique of military expansionism (p. 110).
>
> "Great Law of the Iroquois League" lays out Iroquois conceptions of peacemaking (p. 135).

Treaty Drafting How much authority should the "pen-and-ink work" of written treaties have? How trustworthy are the written texts of past treaties? What about Indian oral tradition and wampum? How binding are either of these forms? Is having a written treaty a useful instrument in making peace? If so, who should draft it?

> The Treaty of Lancaster includes debates about the relative strengths of written, spoken, and wampum forms of agreements between different peoples (p. 70).

Land Cessions: How is ownership of land properly understood? How is ownership properly transferred? Who owns the land to begin with? In particular, should Pennsylvania's 1737 and 1754 acquisitions be respected?

The Treaty of Lancaster includes a debate regarding different justifications for the ownership of territory: conquest, occupation, and purchase (p. 70).

Zeisberger's "Delawares and the Allegheny River Valley" clarifies Delaware claims of ownership of the westernmost portion of the Albany Purchase of 1754 (p. 107).

Indian Politics

Pennsylvania's meddling in Indian politics formed a central component of their attempts to maintain a peaceful frontier for many years. This strategy is likely to continue, but the situation at the outset is unclear. Who among the Indian delegation can lead the way to peace?

Iroquois Hegemony For Indians: Can the Iroquois claim authority over the Delaware? For Pennsylvanians: Should you support Iroquois hegemony or should you deal with the Delaware directly?

The Iroquois first asserted this claim in the Philadelphia Treaty of 1742 (p. 67). It was tacitly accepted by the Proprietors.

"Delaware as Women" describes Iroquois efforts to exert hegemony over the Delawares (p. 151).

Teedyuscung For Indians: Is being a war captain the same as being a chief? Is Teedyuscung too mercurial to be a good leader? Is he too friendly with the whites? For Pennsylvanians: Can you trust a killer? Should Teedyuscung remain the Proprietors' "agent and counsel" among the Delaware?

"Teedyuscung's Raid" describes Teedyuscung's role as a war leader (p. 154).

Making War

Both sides use tactics that the other finds barbaric. Pennsylvania offers bounties for scalps; Indians have executed many of their prisoners. They have also taken members of frontier families captive.

Scalp Bounties Are scalp bounties a legitimate means of war? Does efficacy outweigh the potential for the deaths of innocents or the alienation of allies?

"John Armstrong's Account of the Kittanning Fight" gives a good sense of backcountry warfare (p. 127).

"Deliberations of the Governor's Council" includes a list of scalp bounties (p. 122).

Repatriate Captives For Pennsylvania: Must captured Indians be repatriated? Should Indian adoption rituals be respected? For Indians: Can you relinquish your new family members? Alternatively: Are you ready to forgo the ransoms that the French have been paying for captives?

John Cox's "The Testimony of an Escaped Prisoner," gives a sense of the experience of captivity (p. 133). This document is also a good source of intelligence regarding the current state of the Indian war effort.

Fort Duquesne For Indians: If the fort is taken, a British army will be at the gates of the Ohio Country; is that problematic? For Pennsylvanians: What are the implications of funding and fielding a large army?

Accommodation

Indians and European settlers in this region have been engaged in significant cultural and economic exchanges for decades. Although mutually beneficial in many ways, the general trend has favored Pennsylvanians, and the imbalance of contributions is a factor in the outbreak of war. Everyone needs to consider possible changes in these relationships.

Expansion Should Pennsylvania's government try to stem the westward flow of white settlers? Is a permanent British military presence in the frontier a good guarantor of peace or an irritant that will likely lead to future armed conflict? If peace can be forged, how can it be maintained if white settlers and traders resume their westward march toward Ohio? Consider the overwhelmingly peaceful history of Pennsylvania–Delaware–Iroquois relations; what maintained the peace for so long? Why did it break down?

Heckwelder's "The Coming of Miquon" provides a Delaware account of the first encounter between their people and white men (p. 102).

Trade Should commerce be reopened? Does trade facilitate the dependence of Indians on whites? In particular, what should be done about trade in liquor and guns? Should trade be regulated somehow?

The Carlisle Treaty of 1753 describes the problem of unscrupulous traders (p. 92).

"Deliberations of the Governor's Council" deals with trade issues (p. 122).

Assimilation Is it possible or desirable for Indians to insulate themselves from white influences? Should they try to become more like the whites? Should they welcome Christian missionaries or shun them?

"Great Law of the Iroquois League" lays out the virtues of Indian cultures in general (p. 135).

Pennsylvania Politics

Unlike the previous four issues, Pennsylvania politics does not need to be addressed in the official oratories at the Treaty Council, but it is important, especially for the Pennsylvanians. Particularly canny Indians will consider these issues as well; if they understand them, they may be able to exploit the divisions between the Pennsylvanians.

Quakers Can pacifists be part of government in time of war? Is pacifism tantamount to disloyalty? Are self-proclaimed peacemakers, like Israel Pemberton, muddying the waters or facilitating peace?

Smith's *A Brief State* attacks the Quakers as pawns of the French (p. 112).

Woolman's "Epistle from the Society of Friends" asserts his confidence in pacifism (p. 110).

Proprietary Authority How much prerogative should the proprietors and their employees have? What about the Pennsylvania Assembly? Should the provincial charter (which protects religious liberty) be maintained? Are distant and authoritative proprietors desirable if they guarantee religious liberties, prosperity, and (until fairly recently) peace?

Consider the difference between the outcomes of the Carlisle Treaty (p. 92), in which Pennsylvania was represented by commissioners of the assembly, and the Philadelphia Treaty (p. 67) and Treaty of Lancaster (p. 70), in which Pennsylvania was represented by previous lieutenant governors.

RULES AND PROCEDURES

Objectives and Victory Conditions

This is a game about peacemaking. At the beginning of the game in 1757, Pennsylvania and the Delaware Indians are engaged in a vicious and destructive war, and both sides are weary. Most of the roles advocate peace, but they have other goals as well, like reopening the arms trade or settling disputes over land ownership. Conflicts between these secondary goals makes hammering out a workable peace challenging. Every role sheet describes a unique set of objectives, and everyone who desires peace will need to make some sacrifices, but some roles are more inflexible than others. Remaining true to your role, promoting your understanding of key documents, and grasping the historical context are the crucial factors for success.

It is unlikely that you will be able to achieve every objective listed on your role sheet. If it looks like this is happening at the treaty council, it should be cause for concern rather than celebration because it probably means that other players have achieved very few of their objectives in terms of the treaty. If there are enough of these players, they will undermine the peace during the Coda. This may be done by initiating military operations or by failing to fulfill requirements of the treaty. For example, the Lieutenant Governor may promise to suspend the liquor trade, but if the assembly refuses to pass a law confirming this, the agreement is void. So, it is against your interest to simply ram through a treaty that fulfills only your objectives.

Unless the treaty has broad support, it will collapse and the war will continue. If this occurs, most players lose the game. If peace is forged, victory is possible, but not ensured. Victory goes to those who fulfill more of the objectives on their role sheets than their opponents. It is a delicate balance.

Follow the Protocols

The diplomatic practices of the eastern woodlands of pre-Columbian North America evolved to suit the needs of a diverse world. Communication between different groups was complicated by the multiplicity of languages, but the ascendancy of the Iroquois facilitated the widespread use of the rituals that lay at the mythical heart of the Haudenosaunee, or Iroquois League. These protocols evolved to create a workable structure for forest diplomacy.

The somewhat stilted nature of these protocols actually aided in mutual understanding. The rituals that opened a negotiation lessened the chances of confusion and misunderstanding because they followed a familiar script. Similarly, parsing the negotiation into a deliberate series of oratories increased opportunities for reflection, clarification, and the development of concord.

These well-honed diplomatic customs continued to evolve after the arrival of Europeans in North America. The addition of wampum, gun salutes, toasts, and the distribution of European goods as gifts were important innovations, but tradition remained the guiding force behind the structure of any official negotiations. As historian James Merrell puts it, "Native etiquette set the tone of frontier foreign relations."[1]

Many Europeans who attended treaty councils were eager for the opening ceremonies to end so they could begin working on deals in the bushes. Some did not wait; they began making quiet approaches before the ceremonies even began. It is not entirely disrespectful to engage in these initial informal talks, particularly if players want to shape the agenda that will be laid out in the opening oratory, but Indians should definitely avoid making any commitments before the Treaty Council begins in earnest. Consider the lack of reflection and proper procedure that went into the sale of Iroquois lands to Conrad Weiser in the Albany Purchase of 1754.

Traditionally, Indians focused more on the *process* of negotiation than the *product*, so most of them will be looking to the Lieutenant Governor and the Interpreters to follow the proper protocol as a gesture of good faith. Substantive talks are unlikely if Brother Onas arrogantly flouts the ancient ways. Mutual understanding may be impossible if they cannot grasp matters as elemental as these ceremonies. In addition to sizing up the Pennsylvanians, the opening ceremonies offer the Indians a good opportunity to begin to develop unanimity within their delegation. Without a united front, it will be difficult for them to negotiate a just peace.

For Indians, this deliberate process ideally results in the development of an evolving agreement that periodically gets refreshed at subsequent conferences—that keeps the covenant chain polished and bright. But decades of experience with Europeans and their habit of referencing written treaties as enduring sources of authority over what they see as impermanent spoken agreements have led many Indians to begin to focus as much on the written treaty as on the ceremonies and negotiations that precede it.[2]

The pen-and-ink work of the formal written treaties were the product of the negotiations. These official records were compiled by official clerks. In the case of this Treaty Council, the official clerk is Richard Peters. Once negotiations are committed to writing, they remain available for future consultations. This makes it easy to review the discussion of a subject from an earlier session so that everyone can remember points of agreement and disagreement that have already been established. Similarly, anyone may reference agreements made in earlier treaties from the game book. During the Lancaster Treaty of 1744, the representatives of Maryland and Virginia did this to dramatic effect when they produced old written treaties to support their positions (see p. 70).

---

1. For more on this, see James H. Merrell, *Into the American Woods: Negotiators on the Pennsylvania Frontier* (New York: Norton, 1999), p. 58.

2. Merrell, *Into the American Woods,* chap. 7.

Talks "In the Bushes"

Much of the diplomatic work at the Treaty Council will be accomplished in the bushes—that is, in the informal discussions that come before and after the formal ceremonies and oratory. Once the Treaty Council begins, Interpreters can call a recess for talks in the bushes at any time, but clever players will get a jump on things. Talks in the bushes can begin as soon as the Prelude ends.

Proper Seating

During the Treaty Council, Interpreters must arrange the players into the proper seating arrangement, as follows.

Divide the space in half.

Proprietary officials and commissioners of the assembly sit in chairs on one side.

Richard Peters should sit at an easily accessible clerk's table, which should be fairly large because wampum, maps, and documents may be placed on it. Peters is responsible for compiling an official record of the negotiation. The treaty document he composes is, as far as the Pennsylvanians and the Crown are concerned, the treaty, so it should be as complete as possible. Under certain circumstances, he may be joined at the table by Charles Thomson.

Other Pennsylvanians must fend for themselves.

Indians usually sit on the floor on the other side of the room. Headmen sit in front. Warriors, women, and children sit behind them, and they may move about. If they want to sit on chairs, they may, but it is not really the Indian way.

At least one Interpreter should stand in the middle.

NOTE

Unofficial minutes may be taken by anyone except members of the Indian faction. They are illiterate.

TIP

If confusion or misunderstandings begin to develop, the Interpreters should try to sort it out.

Wampum

During the Treaty Council, every major issue that is brought up in a formal oratory must be represented by a belt of **wampum**. These belts must be made by the Delaware Matriarch. No other player knows how to make them.

Wampum was, in many ways, the product of intercultural interactions. Wampum beads were manufactured by Europeans as a trade good. Indian women then threaded these beads into belts and strings. They did this to facilitate the diplomatic negotiations of their own peoples. They also made wampum when employed to do so by European authorities.

Memory Aids

All of the players in the Indian Faction are illiterate. Consequently, their speeches must be spoken from memory. They cannot use written notes, but they can use wampum, marked sticks, and/or metaphors as mnemonic devices.

> **NOTE**
>
> If the Pennsylvanians begin to feel left out, they may shout, "Huzzah!"

Shout "Yo-Heh!"

Indians should give proper attention when a ceremony or formal oratory is being performed. They must listen closely and without interrupting, but if they like what someone says, they should shout, "Yo-heh!" Europeans recorded this in various ways, including "jo-hah," "yo-ha," "woh," and "wugh."

Gift Giving

Important proposals should be accompanied by a gift (perhaps of wampum). If they are not, or if the gift is of inferior quality, the recipients know that the proposals are not serious ones. Indians may give the Pennsylvanians token gifts, but given the disparity of wealth, these gifts will probably be symbolic. Gifts should be received with a "yo-heh."

> **NOTE**
>
> Israel Pemberton possesses resources that will allow him to offer gifts at the Treaty Council. If larger gifts are promised, the assembly will need to approve appropriations to purchase them during the Coda.

Patronage and Other Side Deals

Side deals are agreements that are made between players who are not mentioned in the official treaty document. These might include exchanges of arms, captives, land, or political favors. It may also include agreements regarding the exchange of patronage tokens. Players must register side deals with the GM before the end of the Coda. The requirements for making a side deal depend on the cultural background of the parties who are making the deal.

If a side deal is between an Indian and a European, it must be committed to writing. To be binding, it must be notarized by an Interpreter before being submitted to the GM. If the deal concerns the transfer of land ownership, it must be accompanied by a map prepared by the Surveyor General.

If the deal is between two Indians, to be binding, they must each make a spoken vow to uphold the arrangement in the presence of the GM and the Matriarch.

If two Europeans strike a side deal it must be committed to writing and submitted to the GM to be binding.

WARNING! *Patronage cannot be converted into cash to buy gifts, weapons, or supplies.*

The most common form of side deal is the extension of patronage. Many Pennsylvanians seek patronage, which represents a combination of friendships and favor trading rather than cash. Essentially, it is a way to get access to the political and financial elite in Philadelphia. Roles that possess sources of patronage may distribute it to those they consider most deserving in the form of "patronage tokens," which are attached to their role sheets.

WARNING! *Patronage cannot be acquired under false pretenses. If the recipient fails to fulfill the conditions set out by the patron, the patronage token is void.*

Patrons may require favors from the recipients of their patronage. After discussing the terms of their agreement, patrons should include a description of the favor on their patronage token. Alternatively, patronage may be extended with no strings attached.

BASIC OUTLINE OF THE GAME

In an effort to reflect historical protocols that governed eighteenth-century treaty councils in the eastern woodlands of North America, the schedule for *Forest Diplomacy* is fairly detailed. The Indians in attendance expect certain things to happen at certain times. If they are disappointed they may walk away.

Prologue

Before the game begins, players usually spend at least two sessions discussing the historical context for the game and the treaties that appear in the game book. Instructors may ask players to take quizzes on these elements. Instructors may opt to create an additional setup session to discuss the other documents or additional historical context.

TIP

After receiving their roles, faction members may meet outside of regular game sessions.

Game Session 1: Prelude

During the Prelude, players divide into three groups: Interpreters, Pennsylvanians, and Indians. The latter two groups meet separately from one another. During these meetings, most players will present their initial speeches. Because Interpreters may move back and forth between cultures, Indians and Pennsylvanians may be able to ascertain some of the positions held by members of the other culture, but they see only through a glass darkly.

TIP

The Pennsylvanians are made up of the Proprietary, Assembly, and Independent factions.

The Pennsylvanians meet "in Philadelphia." The following players should give speeches:

Benjamin Franklin

Anglican Commissioner

Quaker Commissioner

British Major

Israel Pemberton

Surveyor General

Quaker Pariah

The Indians meet "in Diahoga," which is in Iroquois country. The following players should present oratory:

Young Warrior

Lapachpitton

Iroquois Representative

Ohio Chief

Interpreters do not give speeches during the Prelude. They should shuttle back and forth between Philadelphia and Diahoga.

Listening to the speeches given by members of your group is an essential step toward achieving your own objectives because players who share your objectives are likely allies. You can work together during the rest of the game. However, you should recognize that full disclosure is unlikely; many players will reveal some of their aims, but they will conceal others. A few roles are not required to give public speeches at all, which makes their objectives harder to determine, but careful reading of the history and documents will allow you to puzzle out many of their positions.

Game Sessions 2–4: Treaty Council

The structure of formal treaty deliberations is dictated by the traditional rituals of Indian forest diplomacy, which are intended to create a dispassionate space amid the bloodthirstiness of war. It is important to remember that the sessions of the Treaty Council are not debates, rather they are what historian Michael K. Foster describes as a "kind of formal dialogue between the speakers appointed on each side."[3]

3. Michael K. Foster, "On Who Spoke First at Iroquois-White Councils: An Exercise in the Method of Upstreaming," in *Extending the Rafters: Interdisciplinary Approaches to Iroquoian Studies,* Michael K. Foster, Jack Campisis, and Marianne Mithun, eds. (Albany: State University of New York Press, 1984), pp. 184–85.

Treaty protocol dictates that these deliberations will be dominated by formal ceremonies and oratories presented by a handful of roles. These players are charged with following certain ritual forms that provide the treaty with its structure. Understanding and respecting these conventions is an essential element in peacemaking.

First Treaty Council Session Three opening ceremonies set the tone for the Treaty Council and provide a ceremonial beginning to the establishment of one-mindedness. These ceremonies should be accompanied by wampum, which the presenters should procure from the Matriarch. Because the sentiments expressed in these ceremonies are simpler than the proposals in the Treaty Council, this wampum may be in the form of strings rather than belts.

Conrad Weiser presents the Woods' Edge Ceremony to the Indians for the Proprietary Faction

George Croghan presents the Condolences Ceremony to the Proprietary Faction for the Delaware

Turtle Sachem presents the Recitation of the Law Ways

The opening oratory that follows essentially sets the agenda for the entire Treaty Council, so it should be structured as a set of proposals. Once the agenda is set, it may be difficult to squeeze additional issues into the treaty.

Lieutenant Governor presents the opening oratory

Indians acknowledge the oratory and ask for clarifications

TIP

Players may want to talk to the Lieutenant Governor ahead of time to make sure that particular issues make it into his oratory.

Indians should not respond at length. Instead, they should retire to consider what has been said. They need not *formally* reply until the next session, but talks in the bushes may begin immediately.

Wampum The Lieutenant Governor and the Indians who present formal response oratories on the second day of the Treaty Council should punctuate *each* major issue with a belt of wampum, which should be procured from the Matriarch. Wampum belts feature figures and symbols, allowing them to serve as mnemonic devices. Wampum was also a sacred instrument for creating one-mindedness. For an example of wampum's supernatural power, see the "Great Law of the Iroquois League" (on p. 135). The presentation of the wampum belt by the British during the October 2 meeting of the Carlisle Treaty of

WARNING! *If there is no wampum, many Indians may decide that the Pennsylvanians are being insincere.*

1753 (p. 92) is a good brief example of how a belt could embody a relationship between peoples.[4]

Second Treaty Council Session Historically, if the opening oratory was ill-considered, insincere, or rude, the formal reply could be days in coming. Sometimes Indians simply responded to an oratory they disliked with silence. Contrariwise, if an oratory was straightforward and the listeners were already of one mind (or if they anticipated the content of the oratory as a result of talks in the bushes), their response could come after a short consultation. Sometimes it could even come on the same day.

Teedyuscung (and perhaps other Indians) present the response oratory (or oratories)

Proprietary officials acknowledge the oratory and ask for clarifications

Regardless of the quality and tone of the Lieutenant Governor's opening oratory, this session should begin with Teedyuscung offering a response oratory. In it, he should summarize and respond to several of the points raised by the opening oratory from the previous session.

Once Teedyuscung has concluded his remarks, other members of the Indian Faction may speak as well. They need not cover the same ground as Teedyuscung, but by the end of the response oratories, at least one member of the Indian Faction must address *each* of the points raised by the Lieutenant Governor. So if Teedyuscung is the only Indian to speak, he must address *every point* raised in the opening oratory.

> **TIP**
>
> If people forget what was said in the past, they can ask Richard Peters or Charles Thomson to read sections of previous treaties or the previous session's proceedings for reference.

As with the Lieutenant Governor's opening oration, the Indian response to each of the main issues raised in the opening oratory must be punctuated by a belt of wampum, which should be procured from the Matriarch. During the second session, more than the first, wampum plays an important role: it helps everyone remember what had been said before. To make this connection, speakers may point to, touch, or lift up the wampum presented in the opening oratory, which should be on the clerk's table. When responding to a particular point

> **NOTE**
>
> Interpreters are responsible for keeping all of the wampum available for such references.

---

4. For more on wampum in general see, Merrell, *Into the American Woods,* pp. 187–93; Paul Otto, "*Wampum:* The Transfer and Creation of Rituals on the Early American Frontier," in *Ritual Dynamics and the Science of Ritual,* Vol. 5: *Transfer and Spaces,* Gita Dharampal-Frick, Robert Langer, and Niles Holger Petersen, eds. (Wiesbaden: Harrassowitz Books, 2010), pp. 171–88.

from the opening oratory, speakers should present wampum of comparable size and type.

WARNING! *Indians may not consult written notes during the Treaty Council. Given the absence of a written language, Indians often used wampum, marked sticks, and metaphors as mnemonic devices. You may use them this way too.*

Third Treaty Council Session Once all of the Lieutenant Governor's proposals have been addressed by formal response oratories from the Indian Faction, the Indians may begin introducing additional issues for consideration, but there are no guarantees that there will be time for them to be fully addressed (consider the issue of trade that was raised in the last days of the 1744 Treaty of Lancaster). Alternatively, the Indians and Pennsylvanians may want to clarify the specifics of their previous agreements.

To facilitate substantive discussions, the Interpreters should determine the agenda for this final session of the Treaty Council. They should do so with a mind toward clarifying and finalizing agreements. Compared to the first two sessions, the third may be somewhat freewheeling.

Some players may think that a third session of negotiations appears unnecessary because all of the major issues seem to have been resolved to their satisfaction. They might think this because everyone appears to agree with them on important issues. What appears to be a clever compromise may have made the most outspoken players happy, but these players are almost certainly wrong to be so satisfied. The players who appear to agree with them may be planning on causing the collapse of the treaty through military action. Consequently, this session, if nothing else, is good for scrutinizing agreements so that everyone is more certain that their objectives are actually being met.

Game Session 5: Coda

When negotiations conclude, the peace must be kept, but it can be kept only if a significant majority of the players take actions that uphold it during the Coda. Negotiating a clever compromise is one thing, but if the treaty remains disagreeable to a significant number of participants, it will collapse amid renewed violence. However, if enough participants can be convinced that the treaty represents a just peace then it will stand.

The difficulties of keeping the peace are exacerbated by the separation of cultures. As was the case during the Prelude, players are divided into three groups for the Coda. Once again, only the Interpreters may shuttle back and forth between Philadelphia and Diahoga.

Official Treaty Document Once the proceedings of the Treaty Council are concluded, the work of Richard Peters (and possibly Charles Thomson) begins in earnest. As the official clerk, it is Peters's responsibility to draft the official treaty document. It is Thomson's objective to participate in the creation of that document or, alternatively, to publish his own history of the proceedings.

Richard Peters must distribute the final draft of the official treaty document to everyone at least eight hours before the Coda begins. It must be validated with the signature of Conrad Weiser. Any land deals must be notarized by the Surveyor General. The text of the treaty cannot be changed after it is distributed.

The treaty document should open with a list of those who attended the Treaty Council. Beginning with an account of the opening ceremonies, the body of any treaty document should consist of a transcription of the oratories and discussions that take place in the Treaty Council.

The treaty document must include an accounting of any gifts that were given. If the status of any land is changed by the treaty, it should be reflected on a map prepared by the Surveyor General, which should be attached to the treaty. It should be signed by whoever is making any transfer agreements. (The Treaty of Lancaster provides a good model; see p. 70.)

> **NOTE**
>
> If you are playing without a Surveyor General, Richard Peters should prepare the map.

Speeches and Documents To determine the success or failure of the peace, most players will present a second round of speeches to their respective cultures. Many will use these as an opportunity to reflect on the treaty. Most will need to decide whether or not they intend to uphold the agreements that they made during the Treaty Council. In addition, some players will produce written documents, including the official treaty document and political pamphlets.

In Pennsylvania At the outset of the Coda, pamphlets should be distributed by the following players, provided they have secured patronage:

Pamphleteer

Charles Thomson

Christian Delaware

Then the members of the Assembly faction should all give speeches. The commissioners are

Benjamin Franklin

Anglican Commissioner

Quaker Commissioner

Displaced Pioneer

Then the assembly should vote on appropriations and other legislation. This is the point at which they become key players in the game. If the assembly fails to make appropriations promised at the Treaty Council, then those elements of the treaty are void. Furthermore, the assembly may levy taxes to fund the Pennsylvania militia or the Royal American regiment. Proposals require a majority vote from the commissioners of the assembly to become law. The Lieutenant Governor may not veto measures passed by the assembly. Tie votes are decided by a coin toss.

After the assembly has finished voting, Independents should give their speeches. The Independents who will speak are

Israel Pemberton

British Major

Finally, several members of the Proprietary faction will speak. They are

Surveyor General

Quaker Pariah

Lieutenant Governor

Meanwhile, in Diahoga Indians may want to wait for news from Philadelphia before giving their speeches, but the following Indians must begin giving speeches no later than fifteen minutes into the session.

Teedyuscung

Iroquois Representative

Turtle Sachem

Young Warrior

Lapachpitton

Ohio Chief

Matriarch

Interpreters do not give speeches during the Coda. They should shuttle back and forth between Philadelphia and Diahoga.

Side Deals All side deals must be registered with the GM before the end of the Coda. (For details, see p. 46.)

Military Action Most of the Indians are capable of ordering military operations. Command and control is not centralized for the Indians. Every Indian player influences a number of warriors who may be sent into action. These warriors will not go on the offensive unless they are sufficiently motivated by their leaders in the speeches they give during the Coda. Under certain circumstances, the Lieutenant Governor, the British Major, the Surveyor General, and George Croghan are also able to command military forces.

If a significant number of the players who control military forces were dissatisfied enough with the treaty to issue orders that contradict the agreements reached in the treaty, the treaty will fail and the war will continue. However, if a sufficient number of players hold to the treaty, peace is forged. Only the GM knows where the threshold lies.

Players who control military forces should use their final speeches to describe the orders they are giving their men. Because most of the available forces are essentially volunteer formations, these players must lay out a persuasive rationale for whatever course of action they are taking. If they do not, their forces will balk. Some players may be reluctant to present their speeches before they hear news of the disposition of military forces controlled by others, but they should understand if they do not present their speeches, military forces under their influence cannot take any offensive action. Players who control military forces may direct them toward one of three locations: Fort Duquesne, Pennsylvania farms, or Indian towns.

Fort Duquesne Fort Duquesne is a fort in the European tradition; commanding a strategic position at the forks of the Ohio, it is built out of wood and stone, features raised platforms for cannon and firing slits for musketry. Braddock's defeat shows that even a well-supported force of British regulars and colonial militia will have a hard time chopping through the woods and taking the fort. Their vulnerability to ambush means that most now think that Indian auxiliaries are a necessary component of any British expedition to seize the fort.

> **NOTE**
>
> If Fort Duquesne is taken from the French, the captors may decide to install a garrison or dismantle it.

Raids on Farms Indians may opt to lead their warriors on a new round of raids on Pennsylvania settlers. These raids will be joined by Ohio Indians and, perhaps, French troops and Canadians. The most important factor in the success of these raids is probably supplies. If the Delaware receive substantial gifts fewer will die of cold and hunger during the winter. If gifts include arms and ammunition, it will improve their military might. The likelihood of success for these raids is also increased if the assembly fails to make military appropriations or if the Lieutenant Governor orders Fort Augusta dismantled.

Raids on Indian Towns Under certain circumstances, the Lieutenant Governor, the British Major, and George Croghan may order raids on Indian towns in the Ohio Country. Such an expedition would be modeled on the Kittanning Raid (see p. 127). Chances are increased by military appropriations by the assembly, continued control of Fort Augusta, and the seizure of Fort Duquesne. The maintenance of scalp bounties also increases the likelihood of success because they encourage volunteers.

Debriefing

After the final game session, the GM will facilitate at least one session devoted to debriefing. Beforehand, the GM will determine a number of outcomes using die rolls and charts (not included in the game book). Players may then discuss and reflect on the game as a whole.

In addition, the GM will provide copies of selections of the official treaty and other written accounts of the Treaty Council. Players can then discuss the creation, use, and limitations of historical documents.

ASSIGNMENTS AND GRADING

Speeches

Around half of the players give speeches during the Prelude. While Pennsylvanians may bring notes to the podium they must not simply *read* their speeches. This is also true of Indians when they are in Diahoga, but if they present response oratories during the Treaty Council, they must do so without notes. They may use wampum, metaphors, talking sticks, or other mnemonic devices (see p. 46 for details).

> **TIP**
>
> Even though Indians may speak from notes when they are in Diahoga, the other Indians will be impressed if they do not.

A few players do not present speeches during the Prelude. Instead, they make them during the Treaty Council (see p. 48 for details). After the Treaty Council concludes almost every player gives a second report. Most of these are speeches, but a few are pamphlets or letters.

Written Assignments

Speeches, pamphlets, letters, treaty documents, scripts for ceremonies, and the texts of official oratories presented to the treaty council must be submitted to the GM in writing. Over the course of the game, most players must prepare two of these. The default length for each of these is **3–5 pages**. Charles Thomson, the Christian Delaware, The Pamphleteer, and Richard Peters have writing-intensive roles. In most cases, they need to prepare single pamphlets or treaty documents that are **6–10 pages** in length. Your instructor may adjust these requirements.

COUNTERFACTUALS

Alone, the host of issues driving forest diplomacy during the Seven Years' War is quite complex. When the tangled web of Pennsylvania politics, intercolonial relations, and the inner workings of the Iroquois League and the Delaware nation are added to the mix, it becomes nearly mind-boggling so. For this reason, some of the issues have been simplified.

These simplifications are most apparent in the roles that are not directly associated with historical persons. Rather than approximating the positions of specific historical actors these composite roles are designed to represent certain positions. The personal experiences that appear on their role sheets often are based on historical figures, but they are fiction.

Another simplification is the elimination of the land claims of Connecticut's Susquehanna Land Company and Virginia's Ohio Company, which overlapped those of Pennsylvania. The presence of additional sets of colonial actors into an already complicated mix would create great confusion. Sorting out the competing claims among different colonies could be interesting, but it would detract from the heart of the game.

Similarly, Indian politics have been simplified. Several other tribes were affiliated with the Delaware (particularly the eastern Shawnee), but these groups have been dropped from the game for the sake of clarity. The divisions within and between nations of the Iroquois League have also been papered over. Examining the dynamic relations between the Seneca, Mohawk, and other nations makes for a fascinating study, but in early versions of this game the inclusion of this richness proved confusing rather than illuminating. So, in the end, the Indian groups involved with the game are two: the Iroquois League and the Delaware.

Finally, the game makes it possible for the British to launch an attack on Fort Duquesne earlier than they did historically. Had the British war effort not suffered from debilitating mismanagement this would have been possible. However, this option must be approached with caution. A second failed attempt to take the fort might have resulted in severe consequences for British efforts against the French and Indians elsewhere in North America.

PART 4: ROLES AND FACTIONS

INDIAN FACTION

Infuriated by land fraud and enticed by French promises, most of the Indians in the Susquehanna Valley have turned against Pennsylvania. Many are led by **Teedyuscung,** a Delaware war captain. Somewhat surprisingly, he became receptive to the idea of peace talks in the spring of 1756. Subsequently, Israel Pemberton helped arrange an initial treaty council, which was held at Easton in July of that year. There Teedyuscung made it clear that he was open to peace, provided it was accompanied by gifts and recognition of his authority as an important leader. In the hopes that Teedyuscung might bring other chiefs in to talk, former Lieutenant Governor Robert Hunter Morris appointed him "agent and counsel" of Pennsylvania. This marked a startling departure from Teedyuscung's previous station as a mere war leader because it gave him diplomatic authority and potential political power. Forging peace might secure this newfound authority, but it might also lead to its evaporation. As a consequence, some suspect his apparent willingness to negotiate is simply a ruse; meeting in Easton allows the Indians to examine the defensive works around the town. In addition to a good opportunity for reconnaissance, any gifts given to Teedyuscung will strengthen his position as a leader.

> **NOTE**
>
> Unlike some Reacting to the Past games, *Forest Diplomacy* includes very few fully Indeterminate roles; this means that every role includes a range of flexibility and rigidity.

One of Teedyuscung's most eager supporters (at least until fairly recently) is **Young Warrior**. He accompanied several raids in the summer and is interested in accompanying such raids again. He probably came to Easton to survey its defenses and the readiness of the Pennsylvania militia. Suspicious of the intentions of the Pennsylvanians, most of his friends remain camped outside of town. Young Warrior is affiliated with Teedyuscung because of his ability as a war leader, but he does not feel bound by the war captain's decisions. Young Warrior would like to receive gifts of arms and ammunition.

While Teedyuscung is preeminent, several other members of the delegation also possess considerable influence. Several of them appear to be members of the emerging "peace party." Most of them questioned the wisdom of joining the war against Pennsylvania in the wake of Braddock's defeat, but they were swept along with the tide of events and the arrival of war parties from the Ohio Country. In recent months they have begun to talk openly about peace. They are probably motivated by the growing shortage of food, powder, and lead. They would accept supplies from the French, but the French are at the end of a long and tenuous supply line. The peace party was weakened by the initial success of frontier raids, but now, as the weather turns cold again and supplies become increasingly scarce, they have become difficult to quiet.

The rise of the war party forced the **Turtle Sachem** into silence, but he recently rediscovered his voice. In terms of gifts, he is most interested in non-military supplies like blankets. If he receives gifts, he will distribute them to his followers, which will strengthen his position as a leader.

Conrad Weiser once offered **Lapachpitton** Pennsylvania's support to follow Shingas as the "king" of the Delaware. He declined, but he still possesses considerable influence. Believing that the true leaders of the Delaware reside in the Ohio Country, he questions Teedyuscung's authority to lead, but accepts it for now. He may be attending the conference to report back to the chiefs living in the Ohio Country or he may be reconsidering Weiser's offer. Whatever the case, he will undoubtedly represent the position of the traditionalists among the Delaware. Like the Turtle Sachem, he would most likely welcome gifts of blankets.

The **Matriarch** is a also traditionalist. She will strive to establish the "good mind" of harmony and concord within the Indian faction by paying close attention to ceremony and protocol. She is responsible for making the eight treaty belts of wampum the Lieutenant Governor and the Indians will present during the Treaty Council. She cannot receive gifts directly, but if other Indians receive supplies, many of them would doubtless distribute some of their goods to her.

The **Ohio Chief** desires the resumption of the arms trade, the suspension of the liquor trade, and the recognition of Delaware control over the Juniata Valley and the Ohio Valley—both of which are part of the Albany Purchase of 1754. Unlike the eastern Delaware, his people in the Ohio Valley were out of harm's way, so they successfully harvested most of their crops this fall. Consequently, he is most interested in gifts of firearms and ammunition, which he could distribute to the warriors who follow him.

Iroquois League

The interests of the Grand Council will be promoted by one or more **Iroquois Representatives.** Some within the Six Nations of the Iroquois League are pushing to openly align with the British. Others are pro-French. Rather than war, which the Iroquois have avoided since the Grand Settlement of 1701, most Iroquois want to remain neutral so they can receive gifts that will help them renew their hegemony over neighboring Indians, particularly the Delaware. If Pennsylvania acknowledges Iroquois authority, it will strengthen their hand. Consequently, they want to brighten their covenant chain with Pennsylvania.

Interpreters

Conrad Weiser will serve as the official Interpreter for the Treaty Council. He has dealt honestly with Indians in the past, but he is also renowned for cajoling Indians into making unwise agreements (like the Albany Purchase of 1754). Of all the Interpreters, Weiser is the most closely affiliated with the Proprietary Faction because of his long years of service to the Penn family and his rank as a lieutenant colonel of the Pennsylvania militia, but he is trusted by many Indians who call him Tarachawagon. He seeks patronage.

There is also a **Christian Delaware** landowner in attendance. He lives on his farm near Easton. Some of the other Indians do not entirely trust him because of his apparent ease among the whites. Many Pennsylvanians do not trust him because some Christianized Indians have been active in recent raids. Indeed, Teedyuscung was baptized and converted by German pietists, which did not appear to restrain his actions when he led a raid for captives and scalps. He desperately seeks patronage.

Indian relations throughout eastern North America are ostensibly under the purview of Superintendent of Indian Affairs William Johnson. He maintains close relations with the Iroquois from his estate near Albany, in upstate New York, and is frustrated by the independent diplomatic course charted by Pennsylvania. He has dispatched **George Croghan** as his official representative to monitor and, if necessary, intervene in these negotiations. Croghan is an impressive fellow with a real capacity for languages and making deals. He was one of the foremost traders in the Ohio Country until the French arrived and drove him out. Consequently, his finances became overextended and he is now deeply in debt to a number of Philadelphia merchants. It is widely known that if he sets foot in Philadelphia he will be clapped into debtor's prison. He has a multitude of contacts in the Ohio Country and may be able to influence some warriors among the Mingo people (Iroquois settlers in the Ohio Country who do not fully recognize the authority of the Grand Council of the Iroquois in Onondaga). He seeks patronage.

PENNSYLVANIANS

Divisions between Pennsylvanians are even more pronounced than those that plague the Indians. They are divided into three groups. The first two are antagonistic and organized: the Proprietary Faction and the Assembly Faction. The third is a more motley crew and falls under the heading of the "Independents." Most of them will attempt to affiliate themselves with one or more of the Pennsylvania factions at some point in the game.

Proprietary Faction

This treaty conference was called by the newly appointed **Lieutenant Governor William Denny** of Pennsylvania. He is the ranking proprietary official in the colony and previously served as an officer in the British army. His first priority is securing peace with the Indians, but not at the expense of Penn family interests. Because the provincial charter gives the Proprietors sole authority over making deals with Indians (including purchases of land), he will be the sole *official* voice of

Pennsylvania at the Treaty Council. Yet, as a novice in forest diplomacy, many of his ideas remain unformed. During the Prelude, he should listen and learn from his councilors and the other Pennsylvanians. At the beginning of the Treaty Council, he must present the opening oratory for the conference. He may attempt to dominate the subsequent proceedings, but he should recognize that it is impossible to prevent members of the assembly and the Quakers from conducting discussions in the bushes. He possesses and may distribute patronage, provided he is not removed from office by the Penn family.

Lieutenant Governor Denny is accompanied by other proprietary officials. The first is the provincial secretary, **Richard Peters**, an Anglican clergyman. A loyal functionary of the Penn family for decades, Peters knows a great deal about the workings of Pennsylvania's politics and foreign policy. Determined to defend the Penns and to advance his own interests, what he lacks in power he makes up for in knowledge and cleverness. As the official clerk for the Treaty Council, he is responsible for drafting the official treaty document and distributing it before the Coda. This may give Peters an opportunity to manipulate it in favor of his employers. He does not give an initial report. The only constituency he has to please is the Penn family, and they prefer discretion in their placemen. He possesses and may distribute patronage, provided he is not removed from office by the Penn family.

The **Surveyor General** is a major in the Pennsylvania militia. He lives in Easton, where he owns a substantial house as well as improved and unimproved lands. He served in the assembly, but he eventually lost his seat. His foremost desire is victory over France, which he sees as the instigator of the hostile Indians. He believes the defeat of the French is best achieved in the short term with a well-organized militia and a series of forts and in the long term with a well-supported invasion of Canada by British regulars. As a founder of Easton and surveyor general of the province, he is determined to maintain proprietary control over Pennsylvania's land claims. He seeks patronage.

The final possible companion of the Lieutenant Governor is the one remaining Quaker member of the governor's council. The **Quaker Pariah** is a defense Quaker because of his willingness to compromise his faith in terms of the peaceable testimony. Another long-serving Penn family functionary, he maintains substantial ties to his purist brethren despite the frequent denunciations of his co-religionists. Israel Pemberton is his cousin. He possesses and may distribute patronage, provided he remains on the governor's council.

Assembly Faction

The Pennsylvania delegation also includes a contingent of commissioners from the Pennsylvania Assembly. These men have multiple motives, but they are agreed that they resent the authoritarian grasp of the Penns. Legally, they lack authority to engage in official talks with Indians, but because they control Pennsylvania's finances (only they may levy taxes) they are a force to be reckoned with. Because of the parsimony of the Proprietors, almost all of the instruments of war—forts, militia, and scalp bounties—are paid for with funds appropriated by the assembly. If any promises are made during the Treaty Council sessions, the Assembly Faction must still vote for funding during the Coda.

This faction is led by the hawkish imperialist **Benjamin Franklin**. Equally determined to build the power of the assembly and the British Empire as a whole, Franklin has become a determined opponent of the Proprietary Faction, despite his past alliance with them and his friendships with many proprietary officials. The combination of his stature as a scientist-celebrity (he won the coveted Copley Prize for his experiments with electricity), his economic independence (he owns his own printing shop and holds a lucrative post as the deputy postmaster for the colonies of British North America), and his deep knowledge of Pennsylvania politics make him a powerful force. He is an especially hard-nosed politician and he is willing to drop long-standing associations (both the Proprietors and the Quakers once considered him an ally) for tactical advantage. Franklin also possesses a significant amount of experience with Indian negotiations, having served as a commissioner at the Carlisle Treaty of 1753. He also attended the Albany Conference of 1754, where he witnessed Conrad Weiser's masterful manipulation of the Iroquois to the benefit of the Proprietors. He possesses and may distribute patronage.

The first of Franklin's colleagues is a **Quaker Commissioner of the Assembly** from Philadelphia. Like the Quaker Pariah on the Lieutenant Governor's council, he is a defense Quaker who split with his purist brethren because he was willing to fund military efforts. He reluctantly supports armed self-defense, but he may be willing to equivocate further. He possesses and may distribute patronage.

More closely allied to Franklin is an **Anglican Commissioner of the Assembly** from Philadelphia. Active in Indian trading, he wants peace with the Indians, but only if the influence of the French can be eliminated from the Ohio Country. He is a newcomer to the assembly, having secured his seat as a result of the recent resignation of a number of Quaker officeholders. He seeks patronage.

An inhabitant of the frontier, the **Displaced Pioneer** joined the Pennsylvania militia, but the ineptitude of the commanders and poor quality of the equipment and training eventually led him to resign. Like the Anglican Commissioner, he secured a seat in the assembly in the recent election. Because he is seen by many as the voice of the refugees who now clog the streets of Philadelphia, he possesses and may distribute patronage.

Independents

Several roles do not fit neatly into the factions already described. Some of these characters lean toward the Proprietary Faction, while others sympathize with the Assembly Faction.

A recent arrival in Pennsylvania, the **Pamphleteer** is an aspiring literary hatchet man who has made himself known in Philadelphia coffeehouses as a well-read and capable man. Pennsylvania offers such men good prospects for quick advancement. Although many of his positions are unformed, he is enamored of William Smith's recently published anti-Quaker diatribe, *Brief State of the Province of Pennsylvania,* and he wants to follow in Smith's footsteps. Even now he is sharpening his quill. He desperately seeks patronage.

A **British Major** serving as a recruiter for the Royal American Regiment (officially the Sixtieth Royal Regiment of Foot) is also present. He holds a Crown commission as an officer. Consequently, he cannot be issued orders by any Pennsylvania authority. In fact, he may have the ability to issue commands to Pennsylvania militia without the approval of the Lieutenant Governor or the assembly. He is in Pennsylvania in search of funding and support for his regiment, one battalion of which is deployed in Carlisle. He will probably ally himself with whoever offers sufficient enticements. He scorns the idea of receiving patronage from mere provincials.

Many Quakers recently resigned their seats in the assembly after their loyalty began to be questioned by the people of Pennsylvania and the authorities in London. Despite this setback, powerful Quakers continue to influence Pennsylvania's policies. Officially modest when stating their role in treaty negotiations, the Quakers are, in actuality, conducting what amounts to an independent foreign policy toward Indians. These efforts are led by the wealthy and influential **Israel Pemberton**. An important Quaker merchant, he first began to cut a figure in Pennsylvania politics in 1750 when he became the clerk of the Friends' Yearly Meeting in Philadelphia. He served only a single term in the assembly (1750–51), but this did not stop him from becoming known as the king of the Quakers due to his impressive ability to influence fellow Friends. It is important that this influence depends on his powers of persuasion rather than willingness to compromise. As historian Sydney James put it, he is "Intense and passionate, an aggressive champion of virtuous constancy rather than a smooth-tongued master of accommodation."[1] He is particularly inflexible when it comes to the peaceable testimony. He possesses and may distribute patronage.

Although Pemberton has no official role in the proceedings, he possesses two powerful tools that can influence the outcome. The first is money. Quakers paid for the gifts for the Indians at the July conference in Easton. Pemberton has a significant amount of financial support for this conference too. The second is earnestness. Past experience with the lies and evasions of the Proprietary Faction taught Pemberton (and many of the Indians) the importance of good written records. The creation of an independent set of treaty minutes may help keep them honest.

To the latter end, Pemberton is accompanied by **Charles Thomson**. A Presbyterian, he is considered a friend of the Quakers and is attending the conference at Pemberton's request, but he has other friends too. He recently resigned a position

---

1. James, *A People among Peoples*, 158.

at the Philadelphia Academy, which he had secured with the aid of Benjamin Franklin, and it is rumored that he is planning to take a new position as the schoolmaster of the Friends' Charter School in Philadelphia. A massive intellect with a capacity for languages, he is considered by some to be the most trustworthy man in Pennsylvania. He seeks patronage.

PART 5: CORE TEXTS

All players can profit from familiarizing themselves with the following documents, but for every role some documents are more important than others. See your role sheet for more information.

Each document is introduced by a headnote. Most of the documents are glossed with editorial comments that are set off in brackets and italics. Throughout, I silently corrected typographical errors, and in a few cases modernized spelling, but only for clarity.

TREATIES

Philadelphia Treaty of 1742

The treaty at Philadelphia occurred because the Delaware protested the Walking Purchase of 1737. By this point, many Delaware had migrated westward to the Susquehanna River valley, but others remained on the land along the Delaware River conveyed to Pennsylvania by this purchase. The treaty was attended by representatives of Pennsylvania, chiefs of the Delaware, and representatives of the Iroquois League.

This excerpt from the larger treaty shows the forcefulness of the proprietary reaction to this questioning on the part of the Delaware. This is a counterstrike. First, they presented a copy of the written treaty that facilitated the purchase as well as a host of accompanying paperwork. Then, they unleashed Canassatego, a representative of the Iroquois League, who, in the passage that follows first addressed his "brothers," the proprietary of Pennsylvania, and then forcefully demoted his Delaware "cousins" to the status of women and ordered them across the Delaware River.

These actions benefited both the proprietary and the Iroquois. Pennsylvania maintained title to the land, and the Iroquois asserted hegemony over the Delaware with Pennsylvania's assent. Unfortunately for the Delaware, this partnership left them with little room to maneuver. (For more on the concept of the Delaware as women, *see p. 151.)*

SOURCE: *Indian Treaties Printed by Benjamin Franklin, 1736–1762* (Philadelphia: Historical Society of Pennsylvania, 1938).

At a C O U N C I L held at the Proprietor's, *July* 12. 1742.

PRESENT

The Honourable *GEORGE THOMAS*, *Esq;* Lieut. Governor.

James Logan,

Thomas Lawrence,

Robert Strettell,

Clement Plumsted,

Abraham Taylor, Esqrs;

Mr. Richard Peters.

CANASSATEGO, SHICKCALAMY, And sundry Chiefs of the Six Nations.
SASSOONAN, and Delawares. NUTTIMUS, and Fork-Indians.
CONRAD WEISER, Interpreter.
Pisquetoman, Cornelius Spring, Nicholas Scull. Interpreters to the Fork Indians.

CANASSATEGO said:
BRETHREN the Governor and Council,

The other Day you informed us of the Misbehaviour of our Cousins the *Delawares,* with respect to their continuing to claim, and refusing to remove from some Land on the River *Delaware,* notwithstanding their Ancestors has sold it by a Deed under their Hands and Seals to the Proprietaries, for a valuable Consideration, upwards of *Fifty* Years ago; and notwithstanding that they themselves had about [*illegible*] Years ago, after a long and full Examination, ratified that Deed of their Ancestors, and given a fresh one under their Hands and Seals; and then you requested us to remove them, enforcing your Request with a String of Wampum.—Afterwards you laid on the Table our own Letters by *Conrad Weiser,* some of our Cousins Letters, and the several Writings, to prove the Charge against our Cousins, with a Draught of the Land in Dispute [*that is, a map*].—We now tell you, we have perused all these several Papers: We see with our own Eyes, that they have been a very unruly People, and are altogether in the Wrong in their Dealings with you.—We have concluded to remove them, and oblige them to go over the River *Delaware,* and quit all Claim to any Lands on this Side for the Future, since they have received Pay for them, and it is gone thro' their Guts long ago.—To confirm to you that we will see your Request executed, we lay down this String of Wampum in return for yours.

Then turning to the *Delawares,* holding a Belt of Wampum in his Hand, he spoke to them as follows:

COUSINS,

Let this Belt of Wampum serve to Chastize You; You ought to be taken by the Hair of the Head and shak'd severely till you recover your Senses and become

Sober; you don't know what Ground you stand on, nor what you are doing. Our Brother *Onas's* Case is very just and plain, and his Intentions to preserve friendship; on the other Hand your Cause is bad, your Heart far from being upright; and you are maliciously bent to break the Chain of friendship with our Brother *Onas* and his People. We have seen with our Eyes a Deed sign'd by nine of your Ancestors above *Fifty* Years ago for this very Land, and a Release sign'd not many Years since by some of yourselves and Chiefs now living to the Number of fifteen or upwards.

Onas *is the Proprietary of Pennsylvania.*

But how come you to take upon you to Sell Land at all: We conquered you, we made Women of you; you know you are Women, and can no more sell Land than Women; nor is it fit you should have the Power of Selling Lands, since you would abuse it. This Land that you Claim is gone through Your Guts. You have been furnished with Cloaths, Meat and Drink, by the Goods paid you for it, and now you want it again, like Children as you are.

But what makes you sell Land in the Dark. Did you ever tell us that you had sold this Land. Did we ever receive any Part, even the Value of a Pipe Shank, from you for it. You have told us a blind Story, that you sent a Messenger to us to inform us of the Sale, but he never came among us, nor we never heard any thing about it.

This is acting in the Dark, and very different from the Conduct our *Six* Nations observe in their Sales of Land; on such Occasions they give publick Notice, and invite all the *Indians* of their united Nations, and give them a Share of the Present they receive for their Lands.—This is the Behaviour of the wise united Nations.

But we find you are none of our Blood: You act a dishonest Part, not only is this but in other Matters: Your Ears are ever Open to slanderous Reports about our Brethren; you receive them with as much Greediness as Lewd Women receive the Embraces ofbad Men. And for all these Reasons we charge you to remove instantly; we don't give you the Liberty to think about it. You are Women. Take the Advice of a wise Man, and remove immediately. You may return to the other side of *Delaware* where you came from: But we don't know whether, considering how you have demean'd yourselves, you will be permitted to live there; or whether you have not swallowed that Land down you Throats as well as the Land on this side. We, therefore, assign you two Places to go, either to *Wyomen* or *Shamokin*. You may go to either of these Places, and then we shall have you more under our Eye, and shall see how you behave. Don't deliberate; but remove away, and take this Belt of Wampum.

Wyomen *and* Shamokin *are two eastern stretches of the Susquehanna River.*

This being interpreted by *Conrad Weiser* into *English,* and by *Cornelius Spring* into the *Delaware* Language, *Canassatego* taking a String of Wampum, added further.

After our just Reproof, and absolute Order to depart from the Land, you are now to take Notice of what we have further to say to you. This String of Wampum serves to forbid you, your Children and Grand-Children, to the latest Posterity forever, meddling in Land-Affairs; neither you nor any who shall descend from you, are ever hereafter to presume to sell any Land: For which Purpose, you are to preserve this String, in Memory of what your Uncles have this Day given you in Charge.—We have some other Business to transact with our Brethren, and therefore depart the Council, and consider what has been said to you.

Treaty of Lancaster, 1744

*The focus of this treaty is a land dispute between Virginia (*Assaragoa*), Maryland (*Tocarry-hogan*), and the Iroquois League. Pennsylvania (*Onas*) arranged for the treaty to be held in Lancaster, Pennsylvania, in an attempt to play the role of honest broker. Virginia and Maryland agreed to attend because the Iroquois threatened to either attack their frontier settlements or demand direct payment for the land from the settlers. This message had been relayed through Pennsylvania.*

For clarity, I have parsed this treaty into three parts. This does not follow the exact chronology of the treaty, but it does clarify some of the issues and much of the procedure. After several days of pleasantries (which are not reprinted here), the different parties got down to business. Part I concerns the land dispute between Maryland and the Iroquois and features historical disagreements. Part II concerns similar disputes between the Iroquois and Virginia. Here, the argument gets testy as the Iroquois describe their claims of conquest and assert the necessity of having free passage (a "road") south in order to fight their traditional enemies, the Catawba. Finally, Part III acknowledges the resolution to these disputes and provides for the introduction of some additional topics like the renewed hostilities between Britain and France.

Despite the complexity of this treaty (four major participants), it reveals much about the protocol of forest diplomacy. In addition to illustrating the tone, pacing, and structure of an extensive treaty, it shows the importance of talks in the bushes. The speeches allow positions to be established, but they do not allow for much in the way of negotiations—these are conducted in the bushes. The final speeches reveal the establishment of concord.

The second important aspect of the treaty is the disagreement between the various parties about history. Early in the deliberations, the conflict between pen-and-ink work (that is, written treaties) and Indian concepts of oral tradition emerge. When the whites appeared to be getting the upper hand with their references to the considerable paperwork of earlier treaties, Canassatego, who spoke for the Iroquois at the preceding Philadelphia Treaty of 1742, retaliated with his version of history and made an abiding claim on the land that he considers superior to paper: We are from here; you are not. We conquered them; you did not.

Finally, the treaty shows the importance of gifts in maintaining the peace. In the end, despite their protests, both Virginia and Maryland provide the Iroquois with considerable gifts. In return, Iroquois representatives put their marks on two official deeds (one for each colony), which verified the extinguishing of their ownership of land claimed by Virginia and Maryland.

In the following selection, I made some formatting changes for brevity. I have omitted the list of attendees for each phase of the negotiation because, with the exception of the two noted talks with the Maryland commissioners in the court house, those in attendance remained quite constant. I have also removed the discussion of several peripheral issues and some procedural elements.

SOURCE: *Indian Treaties Printed by Benjamin Franklin, 1736–1762* (Philadelphia: Historical Society of Pennsylvania, 1938).

A
TREATY
Held at the Town of *Lancaster,* in Pennsylvania,
By the *Honourable* Lieutenant Governor of the *Province*
Of
PENNSYLVANIA
And the *Honourable* Commissioners of the *Provinces*
Of
VIRGINIA *and* MARYLAND
With the
INDIANS of the SIX NATIONS,
JUNE, 1744.

PRESENT,

The Honourable GEORGE THOMAS, Esq., Lieut. Governor of the Province of *Pennsylvania,* and the Counties of *Newcastle, Kent* and *Sussex,* on *Delaware.*

The Honourable *Thomas Lee,* Esq;
Colonel William Beverly,
Commissioners of *Virginia.*

The Honble Edmund Jennings, Esq;
Philip Thomas, Esq;
Colonel Robert King,
Colonel Thomas Colville,
Commissioners of *Maryland.*

The Deputies of the Onandagoes, Senecas, Cayogoes, Oneidas and Tuscaroraes.

Conrad Weiser, Interpreter.

The council was attended by representatives of all the nations of the Iroquois League save the Mohawks.

* * *

PART I: MARYLAND

he Commissioners of Maryland ordered the Interpreter to acquaint the Indians that the Governor of Maryland was going to speak to them, and then spoke as follows:

Friends and Brethren of the united Six Nations,

WE, who are deputed from the Government of *Maryland* by a Commission under the Great Seal of that Province, now in our Hands (and which will be interpreted to you) bid you welcome; and in Token that we are very glad to see you here as Brethren, we give you this String of Wampum.

Upon which the Indians gave the Yo-hah.

WHEN the Governor of *Maryland* received the first Notice, about seven Years ago, of your Claim to some Lands in that Province, he thought our good Friends and Brethren of the *Six Nations* had little Reason to complain of any Injury from *Maryland,* and that they would be so well convinced thereof, on farther Deliberation, as he should hear no more of it; but you spoke of that Matter again to the Governor of *Pennsylvania,* about two Years since, as if you designed to terrify us.

IT was very inconsiderately said by you, that you would do yourselves Justice, by going to take Payment yourselves: Such an Attempt would have entirely dissolved the Chain of Friendship subsisting, not only between us, but perhaps the other *English* and you.

WE assure you, our People, who are numerous, courageous, and have Arms ready in their Hands, will not suffer themselves to be hurt in their Lives and Estates.

BUT, however, the old and wise People of *Maryland* immediately met in Council, and upon considering very coolly your rash Expressions, agreed to invite their Brethren, the *Six Nations,* to this Place, that they might learn of them what Right they have to the Land in *Maryland,* and, if they had any, to make them some reasonable Compensation for it; therefore the Governor of *Maryland* has sent us to meet and treat with you about this Affair, and the brightening and strengthening the Chain which hath long subsisted between us. And as an Earnest of our Sincerity and Good-will towards you, we present you with this Belt of Wampum.

Next, Maryland challenges the Iroquois land claim, which was made on the basis of the conquest of the Susquehannock. Instead, Maryland's commissioners insist that the land belongs to them, and they present a written treaty to that effect. To solidify their case, they point out that some representatives of the Iroquois approved of Maryland's claims at a treaty in Albany in the late seventeenth century.

On which the Indians gave the Yo-hah.

OUR *Great King of* ENGLAND, and his Subjects, have always possessed the Province of *Maryland* free and undisturbed from any Claim of the *Six Nations* for above one hundred Years past, and your not saying any thing to us before, convinces us you thought you had no Pretence to any Lands in *Maryland*; nor can we yet find out to what Lands, or under what Title, you make your Claim: For the *Sasquahannah Indians,* by a Treaty above ninety Years since (which is on the Table, and will be interpreted to you) give, and yield to the *English* Nation, their Heirs and Assigns for ever, the greatest Part (if not all) of the Lands we possess, from *Patuxent* River, on the Western, as well as the *Choptank* River, on the Eastern Side of the Great Bay of *Cheassapeak*. And, near Sixty Years ago, you acknowledged to the Governor of *New-York* at *Albany,* "That you had given your Lands, and submitted yourselves to the King of *England*."

WE are that Great King's Subjects, and we possess and enjoy the Province of *Maryland* by virtue of his Right and Sovereignty thereto; why, then, will you stir up any Quarrel between you and ourselves, who are as one Man, under the Protection of that Great King?

Finally, the commissioners assert the sovereignty of the king of England, reassert their claims, and insist on their desire for brotherly relations. Then out come the gifts.

WE need not put you in mind of the Treaty (which we suppose you have had from your Fathers) made with the Province of *Maryland* near Seventy Years ago, and renewed and confirmed twice since that time.

BY these Treaties we became Brethren; we have always lived as such, and hope always to continue so.

WE have this further to say, that altho' we are not satisfied of the Justice of your Claim to any Lands in *Maryland,* yet we are desirous of showing our Brotherly Kindness and Affection, and to prevent (by any reasonable Way) every Misunderstanding between the Province of *Maryland* and you our Brethren of the *Six Nations.*

FOR this Purpose we have brought hither a Quantity of Goods for our Brethren the *Six Nations,* and which will be delivered you as soon as we shall have received your Answer, and made so bright and large a Fire as may burn pure and clear whilst the Sun and Moon shall shine.

WE have now freely and openly laid our Bosoms bare to you; and that you may be the better confirmed of the Truth of our Hearts, we give you this Belt of Wampum.

Which was received with the Yo-hah.

After a little Time Canassatego spoke as follows:

Brother, the Governor of Maryland,

WE have heard what you have said to us; and, as you have gone back to old Times, we cannot give you an Answer now, but shall take what you have said into Consideration, and return you our Answer some Time to Morrow. He then sat down, and after some Time he spoke again.

* * *

In the COURT-HOUSE at *Lancaster, June* 26, 1744. *P. M.*

CANASSATEGO spoke as follows:

Brother, the Governor of Maryland,

WHEN you mentioned the Affair of the Land Yesterday, you went back to old Times, and told us, you had been in Possession of the Province of *Maryland* above One Hundred Years; but what is One Hundred Years in Comparison of the Length of Time since our Claim

Canassatego, one of the Iroquois representatives, counters Maryland's references with a lengthy and poetic recounting of the history of European-Iroquois relations.

began? Since we came out of this Ground? For we must tell you, that long before One Hundred Years our Ancestors came out of this very Ground, and their Children have remained here ever since. You came out of the Ground in a Country that lies beyond the Seas, there you may have a just Claim, but there you must allow us to be your elder Brethren, and the Lands to belong to us long before you knew any thing of them.

It is true, that above One Hundred Years ago the *Dutch* came here in a Ship, and brought with them several Goods; such as Awls, Knives, Hatchets, Guns, and many other Particulars, which they gave us; and when they had taught us how to use their Things, and we saw what sort of People they were, we were so well pleased with them, that we tied their Ship to the Bushes on the Shore; and afterwards, liking them still better the longer they staid with us, and thinking the Bushes too slender, we removed the Rope, and tied it to the Trees; and as the Trees were liable to be blown down by high Winds, or to decay of themselves, we, from the Affection we bore them, again removed the Rope, and tied it to a strong and big Rock and not content with this, for its further Security we removed the Rope to the big Mountain and there we tied it very fast, and rowll'd Wampum about it; and, to make it still more secure, we stood upon the Wampum, and sat down upon it, to defend it, and to prevent any Hurt coming to it, and did our best Endeavours that it might remain uninjured for ever. During all this Time the Newcomers, the *Dutch,* acknowledged our Right to the Lands, and solicited us, from Time to Time, to grant them Parts of our Country, and to enter into League and Covenant with us, and to become one People with us.

The "big rock" may refer to the Oneida Country. In which case, "big Mountain" refers to Onondaga, the seat of the Grand Council of the Iroquois League.

After this the *English* came into the Country, and, as we were told, became one People with the *Dutch.* About two Years after the Arrival of the *English,* and *English* Governor came to *Albany,* and finding what great Friendship subsisted between us and the *Dutch,* he approved it mightily, and desired to make as strong a League, and to be upon as good Terms with us as the *Dutch* were, with whom he was united, and to become one People with us: And by his further Care in looking into what had passed between us, he found that the Rope which tied the Ship to the great Mountain was only fastened with Wampum, which was liable to break and rot, and to perish in a Course of Years; he therefore told us, he would give us a Silver Chain, which would be much stronger, and would last for ever. This we accepted, and fastened the Ship with it, and it has lasted ever since.

Canassatego is referring to the English conquest of New Netherlands, which subsequently became New York. The English first conquered New Amsterdam in 1664, and secured the colony by treaty in 1674.

Indeed we have had some small Differences with the *English,* and, during these Misunderstanding, some of their young Men would, by way of Reproach, be every now and then telling us, that we should have perished if they had not come into the Country and furnished us with Strowds and Hatchets, and Guns, and other Things necessary for the Support of Life; but we always gave them to understand that they were mistaken, that we lived before they came amongst us, and as well, or better, if we may believe what our Forefather have told us. We had then Room enough, and Plenty of Deer, which was easily caught; and tho' we had not Knives, Hatchets, or Guns, such as we have now, yet we had Knives of Stone, and Hatchets of Stone, and Bows and Arrows, and those served our Uses as well then as the *English* ones do now.

We are now straitened, and sometimes in want of Deer, and liable to many other Inconveniencies since the *English* came among us, and particularly from that Pen-and-Ink work that is going on at the Table (*pointing to the Secretary*) and we will give you an Instance of this. Our Brother *Onas,* a great while ago, came to *Albany* to buy the *Sasquahannah* Lands of us, but our Brother, the Governor of *New-York,* who, as we suppose, had not a good Understanding with our Brother *Onas,* advised us not to sell him any Land, for he would make an ill Use of it; and, pretending to be our good Friend, he advised us, in order to prevent *Onas's*, or any other Person's imposing upon us, and that we might always have our Land when we should want it, to put it into his Hands; and told us, he would keep it for our Use, and never open his Hands, but keep them close shut, and not part with any of it, but at our Request. Accordingly we trusted him, and put our Land into his Hands, and charged him to keep it safe for our Use; but, some Time after, he went to *England,* and carried our Land with him, and there sold it to our Brother *Onas* for a large Sum of Money; and when, at the Instance of our Brother *Onas,* we were minded to sell him some Lands, he told us, we had sold the *Sasquahannah* Lands already to the Governor of *New-York,* and that he had bought them from him in *England*; tho', when he came to understand how the Governor of *New-York* had deceived us, he very generously paid us for our Lands over again.

Tho' we mention this Instance of an Imposition put upon us by the governor of *New-York,* yet we must do the *English* the Justice to say, we have had their hearty Assistances in our Wars with the *French,* who were no sooner arrived amongst us than they began to render us uneasy, and to provoke us to War, and we have had several Wars with them; during all which we constantly received Assistance from the *English,* and, by their Means, we have always been able to keep up our Heads against their Attacks.

Canassatego acknowledges some of the land purchases that appear in English treaties, but he asserts sovereignty over other lands sold to the colonies by right of conquest.

We now come nearer home. We have had your Deeds interpreted to us, and we acknowledge them to be good and valid, and that the *Conestogoe* or *Sasquahannah Indians* had a Right to sell those Lands to you, for they were then theirs; but since that Time we have conquered them, and their Country now belongs to us, and the Lands we demanded Satisfaction for are no Part of the Lands comprised in those Deeds; they are the *Cohongorontas* Lands; those, we are sure, you have not possessed One Hundred Years, no, nor above Ten Years, and we made our Demands so soon as we knew your People were settled in those Parts. These have never been sold, but remain still to be disposed of; and we are well pleased to hear you are provided with Goods, and do assure you of our Willingness to treat with you for those unpurchased Lands; in Confirmation whereof, we present you with this Belt of Wampum.

Cohongorontas *was another name for the Potomack Indians.*

Which was received with the usual Ceremonies.

CANASSATEGO added, that as the three Governors of *Virginia, Maryland,* and *Pennsylvania,* had divided the Lands among them, they could not, for this Reason, tell how much each had got, nor were they concerned about it, so that they were paid by all the Governors for the several Parts each possessed, and this they left to their Honour and Justice.

* * *

In the COURT-HOUSE at *Lancaster, June* 28, 1744. *P. M.*

In the wake of Canassatego's oratory, Maryland offers to purchase (repurchase?) the lands in question from the Iroquois. They insist on a written deed.

The Commissioners [of Maryland] desired the Interpreter to tell the Indians they were going to speak to them. Mr. Weiser acquainted them herewith. After which the said Commissioners spoke as follows:

Our good Friends and Brethren, the Six united Nations,

WE have considered what you said concerning your Title to some Lands now in our Province, and also of the Place where they lie. Altho' we cannot admit your Right, yet we are so resolved to live in Brotherly Love and Affection with the *Six Nations,* that upon your giving us a Release in Writing of all your Claim to any Lands in *Maryland,* we shall make you a Compensation to the Value of Three Hundred Pounds Currency, for the Payment of Part whereof we have brought some goods, and shall make up the rest in what Manner you think fit.

As we intend to say something to you about our Chain of Friendship after this Affair of the Land is settled, we desire you will now examine the Goods, and make an End of this Matter.

WE will not omit acquainting our good Friends the *Six Nations,* that notwithstanding we are likely to come to an Agreement about your Claim of Lands, yet your Brethren of *Maryland* look on you to be as one Soul and one Body with themselves; and as a broad Road will be made between us, we shall always be desirous of keeping it clear, that we may, from Time to Time, take care that the Links of our Friendship be not rusted. In Testimony that our Words and our Hearts agree, we give you this Belt of Wampum.

On presenting of which the Indians gave the usual Cry of Approbation.

MR. *Weiser* acquainted the *Indians,* they might now look over the several Goods placed on a Table in the Chamber for that Purpose; and the honourable Commissioners bid him tell them, if they disliked any of the Goods, or, if they were damaged, the Commissioners would put a less Price on such as were either disliked or damnified.

Conrad Weiser then coordinates the Indian review of the offered gifts. Initially, the Iroquois appear dissatisfied, but Weiser somehow convinces them to accept Maryland's offer.

THE *Indians* having viewed and examined the Goods, and seeming dissatisfied at the Price and Worth of them, required Time to go down into the Court-House, in order for a Consultation to be had by the Chiefs of them concerning the said Goods, and likewise that the

Interpreter might retire with them, which he did. Accordingly they went down into the Court-House, and soon after returned again into the Chamber.

MR. *Weiser* sat down among the *Indians*, and discoursed them about the Goods, and in some short Time after they chose the following from among the others, and the Price agreed to be given for them by the *Six Nations* was, *viz.*

	L.	s.	d.
Four Pieces of Strowds, at 7 *L.*	28	00	00
Two Pieces Ditto, 5 *L.*	10	00	00
Two Hundred Shirts,	63	12	00
Three Pieces Half-Thicks	11	00	00
Three Pieces Duffle Blankets, at 7 *L.*	21	00	00
One Piece Ditto,	6	10	00
Forty Seven Guns, at 1 *L.* 6 *s.*	61	2	00
One Pound Vermillion,	00	18	00
One Thousand Flints,	00	18	00
Four Dozen Jews Harps,	00	14	00
One Dozen Boxes,	00	1	00
One Hundred Two Quarters Bar-Lead,	3	00	00
Two Quarters Shot,	1	00	00
Two Half Barrels of Gun-Powder,	13	00	00
L.	220	15	00
	Pennsylvania Currency.		

When the *Indians* had agreed to take these Goods at the Rates above specified, they informed the Interpreter, that they would give an Answer to the Speech made to them this Morning by the honourable the Commissioners of *Maryland,* but did not express the Time when such Answer should be made. At 12 o'Clock the Commissioners departed the Chamber.

* * *

In the Court-House at *Lancaster, June* 29, 1744. *A. M.*

After the gifts are accepted, the Iroquois sign away the lands with a written deed.

Mr. Weiser informed the honourable Commissioners [of Maryland], the Indians were ready to give their Answer to the Speech made to them here Yesterday Morning by the Commissioners; whereupon Canassatego spoke as follows, looking on a Deal-board, where were some black Lines, describing the Courses of Potowmack and Sasquahanna:

Brethren,

Yesterday you spoke to us concerning the Lands on this Side *Potowmack* River, and as we have deliberately considered what you said to us on that Matter, we are now very ready to settle the Bounds of such Lands, and release our Right and Claim thereto.

We are willing to renounce all Right to Lord *Baltimore* of all those Lands lying two Miles above the uppermost Fort of *Potowmack* or *Cohongoruton* River, near which *Thomas Cressap* has a hunting or trading Cabin, by a Northline, to the Bounds of *Pennsylvania.* But in case such Limits shall not include every Settlement or Inhabitant of *Maryland*, then such other Lines and Courses, from the said two Miles above the Forks, to the outermost Inhabitants or Settlements, as shall include every Settlement and Inhabitant in *Maryland,* and from thence, by a North-line, to the Bounds of *Pennsylvania,* shall be the Limits. And further, If any People already have, or shall settle beyond the Lands now described and bounded, they shall enjoy the same free from any Disturbance whatever, and we do, and shall accept these People for our Brethren, and as such always treat them.

We earnestly desire to live with you as Brethren, and hope you will show us all Brotherly Kindness; in Token whereof, we present you with a Belt of Wampum.

Which was received with the usual Ceremony. . .

* * *

In the Court-House at *Lancaster, June* 30, 1744. *P. M.*

The honourable the Commissioners ordered Mr. *Weiser* to tell the *Indians* that a Deed, releasing all their Claim and Title to certain Lands lying in the Province of *Maryland,* which by them was agreed to be given and executed for the Use of the Lord Baron of *Baltimore,* Lord Proprietary of that Province, was now on the Table, and Seals ready fixed thereto. The Interpreter acquainted them therewith as desired, and then gave the Deed to *Canassatego,* the Speaker, who made his Mark, and put his Seal, and delivered it; after which, thirteen other Chiefs or Sachims of the *Six Nations* executed it in the same Manner, in the Presence of the honourable the Commissioners of *Virginia,* and divers other Gentlemen of that Colony, and of the Provinces of *Pennsylvania* and *Maryland.*

* * *

PART II: VIRGINIA

In the Court-House at *Lancaster, June* 27, 1744. *A. M.*

The Commissioners of Virginia ordered the Interpreter to let the Indians know the Governor of Virginia was going to speak to them, and they spoke as follows:

Sachims and Warriors of the Six United Nations, our Friends and Brethren,

At our Desire the Governor of *Pennsylvania* invited you to this Council Fire; we have waited a long Time for you, but now you are come, you are heartily welcome; we are very glad to see you; we give you this String of Wampum.

Which was received with their usual Approbation.

The Commissioners of Virginia open negotiations with a more hostile tone than the Marylanders. They testily demand more information about the identity of the Indians that the Iroquois allegedly conquered. They subsequently offer gifts, but they make it clear that they require a quid pro quo before relinquishing them.

* * *

Tell us what Nations of *Indians* you conquered any Lands from in *Virginia,* how long it is since, and what Possession you have had; and if it does appear, that there is any Land on the Borders of *Virginia* that the *Six Nations* have a Right to, we are willing to make you Satisfaction.

Then laid down a String of Wampum, which was accepted with the usual Ceremony, and then added,

We have a Chest of new Goods, and the Key is in our Pockets. You are our Brethren; the Great King is our common Father, and we will live with you, as Children ought to do, in Peace and Love.

We will brighten the Chain, and strengthen the Union between us; so that we shall never be divided, but remain Friends and Brethren as long as the Sun gives Light; in Confirmation whereof, we give you this Belt of Wampum.

Which was received with the usual Ceremony.

TACHANOOTIA replied:

Brother Assaragoa,

You have made a good Speech to us, which is very agreeable, and for which we return you our Thanks. We shall be able to give you an Answer to every Part of it some Time this Afternoon, and we will let you know when we are ready.

In the COURT-HOUSE at *Lancaster, June* 27, 1744. *P. M.*

TACHANOONTIA spoke as follows:

Brother Assaragoa,

Tachanoontia demands to review the letter (which he has his doubts about). He also dismisses suspicions about the Iroquois claims by right of conquest.

SINCE you have joined with the Governor of *Maryland* and Brother *Onas* in kindling this Fire, we gladly acknowledge the Pleasure we have is seeing you here, and observing your good Dispositions as well to confirm the Treaties of Friendship, as to enter into further Contracts about Land with us; and, in Token of our Satisfaction, we present you with this String of Wampum.

Which was received with the usual Ceremonies.

Brother Assaragoa,

* * *

YOU desire to know if we have any Right to the *Virginia* Lands, and that we will make such Right appear, and tell you what Nations of *Indians* we conquered those Lands from.

Now we answer, We have the Right of Conquest, a Right too dearly purchased, and which cost us too much Blood, to give up without any Reason at all, as you say we have done at *Albany*; but we should be obliged to you, if you would let us see the Letter, and inform us who was the Interpreter, and whose Names are put to that Letter; for as the whole Transaction cannot be above a Year's standing, it must be fresh in every Body's Memory, and some of our Council would easily remember it; but we assure you, and are well able to prove, that neither we, nor any Part of us, have ever relinquished our Right, or ever gave such an Answer as you say is mentioned in your Letter. Could we, so few Years ago, make a formal Demand, by *James Logan,* and not be sensible of our Right? And hath any thing happened since that Time to make us less sensible? No; and as this Matter can be easily cleared up, we are anxious it should be done; for we are positive no such thing was ever mentioned to us at *Onandago*, nor any where else.

James Logan was lieutenant governor of Pennsylvania from 1736 to 1738.

All the World knows we conquered the several Nations living on *Sasquahanna, Cohongoronta,* and on the Back of the Great Mountains in *Virginia*: the *Conoy-uch-such-roona, Coch-now-was-roonan, Tohoa-irough-roonan,* and *Connutskin-ough-roonaw,* feel the Effects of our Conquests, being now a Part of our Nations, and their Lands at our Disposal. We know very well, it hath often been said by the *Virginians,* that the *Great King of* ENGLAND, and the People of that Colony, conquered the *Indians* who lived there, but it is not true. We will allow they have conquered the *Sachdagugbroonaw,* and drove back the *Tuscarroraws,* and that they have, on that Account, a Right to some Part of *Virginia*; but as to what lies beyond the

Tachanoontia is describing the practice of adoption, which became common among the Iroquois.

Mountains, we conquered the Nations residing there, and that Land, if the *Virginians* ever get a good Right to it, it must be by us; and in Testimony of the Truth of our Answer to this Part of your Speech, we give you this String of Wampum.

Which was received with the usual Ceremony.

Tachanoontia then becomes magnanimous.

Brother Assaragoa,

We have given you a full Answer to the first Part of your Speech, which we hope will be satisfactory. We are glad to hear you have brought with you a big Chest of new Goods, and that you have the Key in your Pockets. We do not doubt but we shall have a good Understanding in all Points, and come to an Agreement with you.

We shall open all our Hearts to you, that you may know every thing in them; we will hide nothing from you; and we hope, if there be any thing still remaining in your Breast that may occasion any Dispute between us, you will take the Opportunity to unbosom your Hearts, and lay them open to us, that henceforth there may be no Dirt, nor any other Obstacle in the Road between us; and in Token of our hearty Wishes to bring about so good an Harmony, we present you with this Belt of Wampum.

Which was received with the usual Ceremony.

Brother Assaragoa,

Tachanoontia counters Virginia with a reference to a more recent treaty in Albany, which set the location of the Iroquois "road" to the south. He insists that the road cannot be moved westward again.

We must now tell you what Mountains we mean that we say are the Boundaries between you and us. You may remember, that about twenty Years ago you had a Treaty with us at *Albany,* when you took a Belt of Wampum, and made a Fence with it on the Middle of the Hill, and told us, that if any of the Warriors of the *Six Nations* came on your Side of the Middle of the Hill, you would hang them; and you gave us Liberty to do the same with any of your People who should be found on our Side of the Middle of the Hill. This is the Hill we mean, and we desire that Treaty may be now confirmed. After we left *Albany,* we brought our Road a great deal more to the West, that we might comply with your Proposal; but tho' it was of your own making, your People never observed it, but came and lived on our Side of the Hill, which we don't blame you for, as you live at a great Distance, near the Seas, and cannot be thought to know what your People do in the Back-parts: And on their settling, contrary to your own Proposal, on our new Road, it fell out that our Warriors did some Hurt to your People's Cattle, of which a Complaint was made, and transmitted to us by our Brother *Onas*; and we, at his Request, altered the Road again, and brought it to the Foot of the Great Mountain, where it now is; and it is impossible for us to remove it any further to the West, those Parts of the Country being absolutely impassable by either Man or Beast.

"Great Mountain" is probably a reference to the Allegheny Mountains.

We had not been long in the Use of this new Road before your People came, like Flocks of Birds, and sat down on both Sides of it, and yet we never made a

Complaint to you, tho' you must be sensible those Things must have been done by your People in manifest Breach of your own Proposal made at *Albany*; and therefore, as we are now opening our Hearts to you, we cannot avoid complaining, and desire all these Affairs may be settled, and that you may be stronger induced to do us Justice for what is past, and to come to a thorough Settlement of the future, we, in the Presence of the Governor of *Maryland*, and Brother *Onas*, present you with this Belt of Wampum.

Which was received with the usual Ceremony.

Then Tachanoontia *added:*

He forgot to say, that the Affair of the Road must be looked upon as a Preliminary to be settled before the Grant of Lands; and that either the *Virginia* People must be obliged to remove more Easterly, or, if they are permitted to stay, that our Warriors, marching that Way to the Southward, shall go Sharers with them in what they plant.

* * *

In the Court-House at *Lancaster, June* 28, 1744. *P. M.*

The Virginians remain unimpressed. They provisionally accept the Iroquois claims of conquering the Indians who lived in the mountains, but they ask: why haven't we heard this claim before? They argue that this area has been largely uninhabited for some time.

The Commissioners of Virginia desired the Interpreter to let the Indians know, that their Brother Assaragoa was now going to give his Reply to their Answer to his first Speech, delivered them the Day before in the forenoon.

Sachims and Warriors of the united Six Nations,

We are now come to answer what you said to us Yesterday, since what we said to you before on the Part of the Great King, our Father, has not been satisfactory. You have gone into the old Times, and so must we. It is true that the Great King holds *Virginia* by Right of Conquest, and the Bounds of that Conquest to the Westward is the Great Sea.

If the *Six Nations* have made any Conquest over *Indians* that may at any Time have lived on the West-side of the Great Mountains of *Virginia*, yet they never possessed any Lands there that we have ever heard of. That Part was altogether deserted, and free for any People to enter upon, as the People of *Virginia* have done, by Order of the Great King, very justly, as well by an ancient Right, as by its being freed from the Possession of any other, and from any Claim even of you the *Six Nations*, our Brethren, until within these eight Years. The first Treaty between the Great King, in Behalf of his Subjects of *Virginia*, and you, that we can find, was made at *Albany*, by Colonel *Henry Coursey*, Seventy Years since; this was a Treaty of Friendship, when the first Covenant Chain was made, when we and you became Brethren.

The next Treaty was also at *Albany*, above Fifty-eight Years ago, by the Lord *Howard*, Governor of *Virginia*: then you declare yourselves Subjects to the Great King, our

Father, and gave up to him all your Lands for his Protection. This you own in a Treaty made by the Governor of *New-York* with you at the same Place in the Year 1687, and you express yourselves in these Words, "Brethren, you tell us the King of *England* is a very great King, and why should not you join with us in a very just Cause, when the *French* join with our Enemies in an unjust Cause? O Brethren, we see the Reason of this; for the *French* would fain kill us all, and when that is done, they would carry all the Beaver Trade to *Canada,* and the *Great King of* ENGLAND would lose the Land likewise; and therefore, O Great Sachim, beyond the Great Lakes, awake, and suffer not those poor *Indians,* that have given themselves and their Lands under your Protection, to be destroyed by the *French* without a Cause."

THE last Treaty we shall speak to you about is that made at *Albany* by Governor *Spotswood,* which you have not recited as it is: For the white People, your Brethren of *Virginia,* are, in no Article of that Treaty, prohibited to pass, and settle to the Westward of the Great Mountains. It is the *Indians,* tributary to *Virginia,* that are restrained, as you and your tributary *Indians* are from passing to the Eastward of the same Mountains, or to the Southward of *Cohongorooton,* and you agree to this Article in these Words; "That the Great River of *Potomack,* and the high Ridge of Mountains, which extend all along the Frontiers of *Virginia* to the Westward of the present Settlements of that Colony, shall be fore ever the established Boundaries between the *Indians* subject to the Dominions of *Virginia,* and the *Indians* belonging and depending on the *Five Nations*; so that neither our *Indians* shall not, on any Pretense whatsoever, pass to Northward or Westward of the said Boundaries, without having to produce a Passport under the Hand and Seal of the Governor or Commander in Chief of *Virginia*; nor your *Indians* to pass to the Southward or Eastward of the said Boundaries, without a Passport in like Manner from the Governor or Commander in Chief of *New-York.*"

Here, the Virginians make an important observation about the treaty cited by the Iroquois regarding westward expansion and the road. Furthermore, they assert their power over the Iroquois.

AND what Right can you have to Lands that you have no Right to walk upon, but upon certain Conditions? It is true, you have not observed this Part of the Treaty, and your Brethren of *Virginia* have not insisted upon it with a due Strictness, which has occasioned some Mischief.

After citing these treaties, the Virginians insist on the ultimate authority of the written word.

THIS Treaty has been sent to the Governor of *Virginia* by Order of the Great King, and is what we must rely on, and, being in Writing, is more certain than your Memory. That is the Way the white People have of preserving Transactions of every Kind, and transmitting them down to their Childrens Children for ever, and all Disputes among them are settled by this faithful kind of evidence, and must be the Rule between the Great King and you. This Treaty your Sachims and Warriors signed some Years after the same Governor *Spotswood,* in the Right of the Great King, had been, with some People of *Virginia,* in Possession of these very Lands, which you have set up your late Claim to.

In closing, the Virginians invoke the power and authority of the king of England, who they dexterously refer to as "our common father" in an effort to extend his sovereignty over the Iroquois.

Brethren,

THIS Dispute is not between *Virginia* and you; it is setting up your Right against the Great King, under whose Grants the People you complain of are settled. Nothing but a Command from the Great King can remove them; they are too powerful to be removed by any Force of you, our Brethren; and the Great King, as our common Father, will do equal Justice to all his Children; wherefore we do believe they will be confirmed in their Possessions.

Finally, the Virginians close with an insistence on their devotion to peace and a note that the Iroquois are not alone in pressing claims over the land in question.

WE may proceed to settle what we are to give you for any Right you may have, or have had to all the Lands to the Southward and Westward of the Lands of your Brother the Governor of *Maryland,* and of your Brother *Onas*; tho' we are informed that the Southern *Indians* claim these very Lands that you do.

WE are desirous to live with you, our Brethren, according to the old Chain of Friendship, to settle all these Matters fairly and honestly; and, as a Pledge of our Sincerity, we give you this Belt of Wampum.

Which was received with the usual Ceremony.

* * *

In the COURT-HOUSE at *Lancaster, June* 30, 1744. *A. M.*

Gacharadodow begins with a short and acerbic comment about cultural relativism and the will of God. He quickly dismisses the Virginian claim that the Iroquois are the subjects of the king of England and then suggests that the Virginians trot out the gifts.

Gacharadodow, Speaker for the Indians, in Answer to the Commissioners Speech at the last Meeting, with a strong Voice, and proper Action, spoke as follows:

Brother Assaragoa,

THE World at the first was made on the other Side of the Great Water different from what it is on this Side, as may be known from the different Colours of our Skin, and of our Flesh, and that which you call Justice may not be so amongst us; you have your Laws and Customs, and so have we. The Great King might send you over to conquer the *Indians,* but it looks to us that God did not approve of it; if he had, he would not have placed the Sea where it is, as the Limits between us and you.

Brother Assaragoa,

THO' great Things are well remembered among us, yet we don't remember that we were ever conquered by the Great King, or that we have been employed by the Great King to conquer others; if it was so, it is beyond our Memory. We do remember we were employed by *Maryland* to conquer the *Conestogoes,* and that the second time we were at War with them, we carried them all off.

* * *

Brother Assaragoa,

YOU know very well, when the white People came first here they were poor; but now they have got our Lands, and are by them become rich, and we are now poor; what little we have had for the Land goes soon away, but the Land lasts for ever. You told us you had brought with you a Chest of Goods, and that you have the Key in your Pockets; but we have never seen the Chest, nor the Goods that are said to be in it; it may be small, and the Goods few; we want to see them, and are desirous to come to some Conclusion. We have been sleeping here these ten Days past, and have not done any thing to the Purpose.

* * *

THE Commissioners told them they should see the Goods on *Monday.*

* * *

In the COURT-HOUSE at *Lancaster, July* 2, 1744 *P. M.*

The Indians being told, by the Interpreter, that their Brother Assaragoa was going to speak to them, the Commissioners spoke as follows:

The Virginians stand by their argument regarding the rightful ownership of the land, but they begin making concessions. First they snippily present the gifts; then they agree to honor past agreements regarding the road.

Sachims and Warriors, our Friends and Brethren,

As we have already said enough to you on the Subject of the Title to the Lands you claim from *Virginia,* we have no Occasion to say any thing more to you on that Head, but come directly to the point.

WE have opened the Chest, and the Goods are now here before you; they cost Two Hundred Pounds *Pennsylvania* Money, and were bought by a Person recommended to us by the Governor of *Pennsylvania* with ready Cash. We ordered them to be good in their Kinds, and we believe they are so. These Goods, and Two Hundred Pounds in Gold, which lie on the Table, we will give you, our Brethren of the *Six Nations,* upon Condition that you immediately make a Deed recognizing the King's Right to all the Lands that are, or shall be, by his Majesty's Appointment in the Colony of *Virginia.*

As to the Road, we agree you shall have one, and the Regulation is in Paper, which the Interpreter now has in his Custody to show you. The People of *Virginia* shall perform their Part, if you and your *Indians* perform theirs; we are your Brethren, and will do no Hardships to you, but, on the contrary, all the Kindness we can.

THE *Indians* agreed to what was said, and *Canassatego* desired they would represent their Case to the King, in order to have a further Consideration when the Settlement increased much further back. To which the Commissioners agreed, and promised they would make such a Representation faithfully and honestly; and, for their further Security that they would do so, they would give them a Writing, under their Hands and Seals, to that Purpose.

Canassatego wanted the king of England to arbitrate the disagreement over westward expansion. The Virginians agreed to convey a message to him.

Canassatego requested additional gifts, and the Virginians agreed to provide them.

They desired that some Rum might be given them to drink on their Way home, which the Commissioners agree to, and paid them in Gold for that Purpose, and the Carriage of their Goods from *Philadelphia*, Nine Pounds, Thirteen Shillings, and Three-pence, *Pennsylvania* Money.

Canassatego further said, That as their Brother *Tocarry-hogan* sent them Provision on the Road here, which kept them from starving, he hoped their Brother *Assaragoa* would do the same for them back, and have the Goods he gave them carried to the usual Place; which the Commissioners agreed to, and ordered Provisions and Carriages to be provided accordingly.

Finally, the Iroquois signed a land deed conveying the land to Virginia.

After this Conference the Deed was produced, and the Interpreter explained it to them; and they, according to their Rank and Quality, put their Marks and Seals to it in the Presence of several Gentlemen of *Maryland, Pennsylvania* and *Virginia*; and when they delivered the Deed, *Canassatego* delivered it for the Use of their Father, the Great King, and hoped he would consider them; on which the Gentlemen and *Indians* then present gave three Shouts.

PART III: CONCLUSIONS

In the Court-House at *Lancaster, July* 3, 1744 *A. M.*

The Governor spoke as follows:

At the end of the treaty, the governor of Pennsylvania provides a summing up.

Friends and Brethren of the Six Nations,

At a Treaty held with many of the Chiefs of your Nations Two Years ago, the Road between us was made clearer and wiser; our Fire was enlarged, and our Friendship confirmed by an Exchange of Presents, and many other mutual good offices.

We think ourselves happy in having been instrumental to your meeting with our Brethren *Virginia* and *Maryland*; and we persuade ourselves, that you, on your Parts, will always remember it as an Instance of our Goodwill and Affection for you. This has given us an Opportunity of seeing you sooner than perhaps we should otherwise have done; and, as we are under mutual Obligations by Treaties, we to hear with our Ears for you, and you to hear with your Ears for us, we take this Opportunity to inform you of what very nearly concerns us both.

* * *

I need not put you in mind how much *William Penn* and his Sons have been your Friends, and the Friends of all the *Indians*. You have long and often experienced their Friendship for you; nor need I repeat to you how kindly you were treated, and what valuable Presents were made to you Two Years ago by the Governor, the Council, and the Assembly, of *Pennsylvania*. The Sons of *William Penn* are all now in *England*, and have left me in their Place, well knowing how much I regard you and all the *Indians.* As a fresh Proof of this, I have left my House, and am come thus far to see you, to renew our Treaties, to brighten the Covenant Chain, and to confirm our Friendship with you. In Testimony whereof, I present you with this Belt of Wampum.

Which was received with the Yo-ha.

As your Nations have engaged themselves by Treaty to assist us, your Brethren of *Pennsylvania,* in case of a War with the *French,* we do not doubt but you will punctually perform an Engagement so solemnly entered into. A War is now declared, and we expect that you will not suffer the *French,* or any of the *Indians* in Alliance with them, to march through our Country to disturb any of our Settlements; and that you will give us the earliest and best Intelligence of any Designs that may be formed by them to our Disadvantage, as we promise to do of any that may be to yours. To enforce what I have now said to you in the strongest Manner, I present you with this Belt of Wampum.

The governor then encourages the Iroquois to assist the English against the French.

The governor then informs the Indians that England has gone to war against France and Spain and describes victories against them on land and at sea (omitted from this text), and conjures the memories of William Penn.

Which was received with the Yo-ha.

After a little Pause his Honour, the GOVERNOR, spoke again:

Friends and Brethren of the Six Nations,

WHAT I have now said to you is in Conformity to Treaties subsisting between the Province of which I am Governor and your Nations. I now proceed, with the Consent of the honourable Commissioners for *Virginia* and *Maryland,* to tell you, that all Differences having been adjusted, and the Roads between us and you made quite clear and open, we are ready to confirm our Treaties with your Nations, and establish a Friendship that is not to end, but with the World itself. And, in Behalf of the Province of *Pennsylvania,* I do, by this fine Belt of Wampum, and a Present of Goods, to the Value of Three Hundred Pounds, confirm and establish the said Treaties of Peace, Union and Friendship, you on your Parts doing the same.

Then, the representatives of each of the three colonies provide a short, optimistic concluding statement about the value of everlasting friendship. The lieutenant governor of Pennsylvania begins.

Which was received with a loud Yo-ha.

THE Governor further added, The Goods bought with the One Hundred Pounds Sterling, put into my Hands by the Governor of *Virginia,* are ready to be delivered when you please. The Goods bought and sent up by the People of the Province of *Pennsylvania,* according to the List which the Interpreter will explain, are laid by themselves, and are likewise ready to be delivered to you at your own time.

After a little Pause the Commissioners of Virginia spoke as follows:

Sachems and Warriors of the Six Nations,

The Way between us being made smooth by what passed Yesterday, we desire now to confirm all former Treaties made between *Virginia* and you, our Brethren of the *Six Nations,* and to make our Chain of Union and Friendship as bright as the sun, that it may not contract any more Rust for ever; that our Children's Children may rejoice at, and confirm what we have done; and that you and your Children may not forget it, we give you One Hundred Pounds in Gold, and this Belt of Wampum.

Which was received with the usual Ceremony.

* * *

Then the Commissioners of Maryland spoke as follows:

Friends and Brethren, the Chiefs or Sachims of the Six united Nations

As the Treaty now made concerning the Lands in *Maryland* will, we hope, prevent effectually every future Misunderstanding between us on that Account, we will now bind faster the Links of our Chain of Friendship by a Renewal of all our former Treaties; and that they may still be the better secured, we shall present you with One Hundred Pounds of Gold.

What we have further to say to you is, Let not our Chain contract any Rust; whenever you perceive the least Speck, tell us of it, and we will make it clean. This we also expect of you, that it may always continue so bright as our Generation may see their Faces in it; and, in Pledge of the Truth of what we have now spoken, and our Affection to you, we give you this Belt of Wampum.

Which was received with the usual Ceremony.

CANASSATEGO, in return, spoke as follows:

Brother Onas, Assaragoa, *and* Tocarry-hogan,

We return you Thanks for your several Speeches, which are very agreeable to us. They contain Matters of such great Moment, that we propose to give them a very serious Consideration, and to answer them suitably to their Worth and Excellence; and this will take till To-morrow Morning, and when we are ready we will give you due Notice.

You tell us you beat the *French*; if so, you must have taken a great deal of Rum from them, and can the better spare us some of that Liquor to make us rejoice with you in the Victory.

The Governor and Commissioners ordered a Dram of Rum to be given to each in a small Glass, calling it, *A French Glass*.

In the COURT-HOUSE at *Lancaster, July* 4, 1744 *A. M.*

CANASSATEGO Speaker.

On the last day, in parting, Canassatego affirms the good wishes of Pennsylvania, Virginia, and Maryland and offers his understanding of the relationship between the Iroquois and the English in time of war.

ESTERDAY, you expressed your Satisfaction in having been instrumental to our meeting with our Brethren of *Virginia and Maryland*. We, in return assure you that we have great Pleasure in this Meeting, and thank you for the Part you have had in bringing us together, in order to create a good Understanding, and to clear the Road; and, in Token of our Gratitude, we present you with this String of Wampum.

Which was received with the usual Ceremony.

Brother Onas,

You was pleased Yesterday to inform us, "That War had been declared between the *Great King of* ENGLAND and the *French* King; that two great Battles had been fought, one by Land, the other at Sea; with many Particulars." We are glad to hear the Arms of the King of *England* were successful, and take part with you in your Joy on this Occasion. You then came nearer Home, and told us, "You had left your House, and were come thus far on Behalf of the whole People of *Pennsylvania* to see us; to renew your Treaties; to brighten the Covenant Chain, and to confirm your Friendship with us." We approve this Proposition; we thank you for it. We own, with pleasure, that the Covenant Chain between us and Pennsylvania is of old Standing, and has never contracted any Rust; we wish it may always continue as bright as it has done hitherto; and, in Token of the Sincerity of our Wishes, we present you with this Belt of Wampum.

Which was received with the Yo-hah.

Brother Onas,

You was pleased Yesterday to remind us of our mutual Obligation to assist each other in case of a War with the *French*, and to repeat the Substance of what we ought to do by our Treaties with you; and that as a war had been already entered into with the *French*, you called upon us to assist you, and not to suffer the *French* to march through our Country to disturb any of your Settlements.

In answer, We assure you that we have all these Particulars in our Hearts; they are fresh in our Memory. We shall never forget that you and we have but one Heart, one Head, one Eye, one Ear, and one Hand. We shall have all your Country under our Eye, and take all the Care we can to prevent any Enemy from coming into it; and, in Proof of our Care, we must inform you, that before we came here, we told *Onantio*, our Father, as he is called, that neither he, nor any of his People, should come through our Country, to hurt our Brethren, the *English*, or any of the settlements belonging to them; there was room enough at sea to fight, there he might do as

Onantio *was what the Iroquois called the French governor of Canada. Note that he is their "father," while the colonies are "brothers."*

he pleased, but he should not come upon our Land to do any Damage to our Brethren. And you may depend upon us using our utmost Care to see this effectively done; and, in Token of our Sincerity, we present you with this Belt of Wampum.

Which was received with the usual Ceremony.

The Six Nations have a great Authority and Influence over sundry Tribes of *Indians* in Alliance with the *French*, and particularly over the Praying *Indians* formerly a Part with ourselves, who stand in the very Gates of the *French*; and, to show our further Care, we have engaged these very Indians; and other *Indian* Allies of the French for you. They will not join the *French* against you. They have agreed with us before we set out. We have put the spirit of Antipathy against the *French* in those People. Our Interest is very Considerable with them, and many other Nations, and as far as ever it extends, we shall use it for your Service.

After clarifying the form of Iroquois assistance to the English, Canassatego expresses his satisfaction that the foundation for a lasting peace has been laid.

Brother Assaragoa;

You told us Yesterday that all Disputes with you being now at an End; you desired to confirm all former Treaties between *Virginia* and us, and to make our Chain of Union as bright as the Sun.

We agree very heartily with you in these Propositions; we thank you for your good Inclinations; we desire you will pay no Regard to any idle stories that may be told to our Prejudice. And, as the dispute about the Land is now entirely over, and we perfectly reconciled, we hope, for the future, we shall not act towards each other but as becomes Brethren and hearty Friends.

We are very willing to renew the Friendship with you, and to make it as firm as possible, for us and our Children with you and your Children to the last Generation, and we desire you will imprint these Engagements on your Hearts in the strongest Manner; and, in Confirmation that we shall do the same, we give you this Belt of Wampum.

Which was received with Yo-hah from the Interpreter and all the Nations.

Brother Tocarry-hogan,

You told us yesterday that since there was now nothing in Controversy between us, and the Affair of the Land was settled to your Satisfaction, your would now brighten the Chain of Friendship which hath subsisted between you and us ever since we became Brethren; we are well pleased with the Proposition, and we thank you for it; we also are inclined to renew all Treaties, and keep a good Correspondence with you. You told us further, if ever we should perceive the Chain had contracted any Rust, to let you know, and you would take care to take the Rust out, and preserve it bright. We agree with you in this, and shall, on our Parts, do everything to preserve a good Understanding, and to live in the same Friendship with you as our brother *Onas* and *Assaragoa*; in Confirmation whereof, we give you this Belt of Wampum.

On which the usual cry of Yo-hah was given.

* * *

Brother Onas, Assaragoa, *and* Tocarry-hogan,

At the close of your respective Speeches Yesterday, you made us very handsome Presents, and we should return you something suitable to your Generosity; but, alas, we are poor, and shall ever remain so, as long as there are so many *Indian* Traders among us. Theirs and the white Peoples Cattle have eat up all the Grass, and made Deer scarce. However, we have provided a small Present for you, and tho' some of you gave us more than others, yet as you are all equally our Brethren, we shall leave it to you to divide it as you please—and then presented three Bundles of Skins, which were received with the usual Ceremony from the three Governments.

Canassatego offers some reciprocal gifts, and then raises an ancillary issue: trade.

* * *

The Governor replied:

The honourable Commissioners of *Virginia* and *Maryland* have desired me to speak for them; therefore I, in Behalf of those Governments, as well as the Province of *Pennsylvania*, return you Thanks for the many Proofs you have given in your Speeches of your Zeal for the Service of your Brethren the *English*, and in particular for your having so early engaged in a Neutrality the several Tribes of Indians in the *French* Alliance. We do not doubt that you will faithfully discharge your Promises. As to your presents, we never estimate these things by their real Worth, but by the Disposition of the Giver. In this Light we accept them with great Pleasure, and put a high Value upon them. We are obliged to you for recommending Peace and good Agreement amongst ourselves. We are all subjects, as well as you, of the Great King beyond the Water; and, in Duty to his Majesty, and from the good Affection that we bear to each other, as well as from a Regard to our own Interest, we shall always be inclined to live in Friendship.

Then the Commissioners of Virginia presented the Hundred Pounds in Gold, together with a Paper, containing a Promise to recommend the *Six Nations* for further Favor to the King; which they received with *Yo-hah*, and the Paper was given by them to *Conrad Weiser* to keep for them. The Commissioners likewise promised that their public Messengers should not be molested in their Passage through *Virginia* . . .

Then the Commissioners of *Maryland* presented their Hundred Pounds in Gold, which was likewise received with the *Yo-hah*.

Canassatego said, We mentioned to you Yesterday the Booty you had taken from the *French*, and asked you for some of the Rum which we supposed to be Part of it, and you gave us some, but it turned out unfortunately that you gave us it in *French* Glasses, we now desire that you give us some in *English* Glasses.

The deal is sealed with a toast of rum.

The Governor made answer, We are glad to hear that you have such a Dislike for what is *French*. They cheat you in your Glasses, as well as in everything else. You must consider we are at a Distance from *Williamsburg, Annapolis*, and *Philadelphia*, where our Rum Stores are, and that altho' we brought up a good Quantity with us, you have almost drunk it out, but notwithstanding this, we have enough left to fill our *English* Glasses, and will show the Difference between the Narrowness of the *French*, and the Generosity of your Brethren the *English* towards you.

THE Indians gave, in their Order, five *Yo-hahs*; and the honorable Governor and commissioners calling for some Rum, and some middle-sized Wine Glasses, drank health to the *Great King of* ENGLAND and the *Six Nations*, and put an end to the Treaty by three loud Huzza's, in which all the Company joined.

IN the Evening the governor went to take his Leave of the *Indians*, and, presenting them with a String of Wampum, he told them, that was in return for one he had received of them, with a Message to desire the Governor of *Virginia* to suffer their Warriors to go through *Virginia* unmolested, which was rendered unnecessary by the present Treaty.

* * *

The Indians received these two Strings of Wampum with the usual Yo-hah.

* * *

THE Commissioners of *Virginia* gave *Canassatego* a Scarlet Camblet Coat; and took their Leave of them in Form, and at the same time delivered the Passes to them, according to their Request.

THE Commissioners of *Maryland* presented *Gachradodow* with a broad Gold-laced Hat, and took their Leave of them in a similar Manner.

A true Copy, compared by RICHARD PETERS, Secry.

THE END

Carlisle Treaty of 1753

Framed as a report to the lieutenant governor of Pennsylvania, this treaty council was held in Carlisle, Pennsylvania. It was precipitated by the arrival of a large Indian delegation from the Ohio Country in Winchester, Virginia. Because representatives from Virginia met with the delegation it seemed imperative, given disagreement over claims to the Ohio Country, for Pennsylvania to meet with them as well. The delegation included the representatives of a number of peoples. The Delaware, Shawonese or Shawne, Twightwee, and Owendaet all came in strength. The Delaware included the recently named "king" Shingas.

Shingas had taken this new honor fairly recently. At the 1752 treaty between Virginia and the Ohio Indians at Logstown, Tanaghrisson, a Seneca chief who lived in the Ohio Country and oversaw the Ohio Indians for the Grand Council of the Iroquois League at Onondaga, recognized Shingas as the preeminent chief, or king, of the Delaware. The selection of Shingas was preordained, but by confirming the authority of Shingas, Tanaghrisson deftly maneuvered to leave the door open for a future exercise of Iroquois power over the Delaware.

On the Pennsylvania side, the principals were three commissioners: Isaac Norris, the Quaker speaker of the assembly; Benjamin Franklin, a leading member of the assembly; and Richard Peters, the provincial secretary. The latter two gentlemen are in attendance at the treaty council in the game. Clearly out of their depth, they turn the proceedings over to Scarrooyady, a Mingo chief who presented himself as the representative of the Six Nations of the Iroquois League. Like Tanaghrisson, he was a clever diplomat who inflated his authority by associating it and the Iroquois League with the power of Pennsylvania. He translated speeches by the other Indians into English and played a critical role for both sides because the Pennsylvania commissioners entrusted him with the important task of presenting their condolences. In doing so, he brightened the covenant chain between the Iroquois and Pennsylvania.

This treaty provides an excellent example of the importance of condolence rituals. The commissioners repeatedly stressed the need for urgency, but without the proper gifts and rituals, the Indians refused to open the treaty council. Once the proper gifts and a very nice belt of wampum arrived, the orations began. The latter days of the treaty allow time for the Indians to express frustration regarding unscrupulous traders.

For purposes of brevity, I removed several issues and the oration of the Twightwee from this selection.

SOURCE: *Indian Treaties Printed by Benjamin Franklin, 1736–1762* (Philadelphia: Historical Society of Pennsylvania, 1938).

To the Honourable JAMES HAMILTON, Esq; Lieutenant-Governor, and Commander in Chief, of the Province of Pennsylvania, and Counties of New-Castle, Kent and Sussex, upon Delaware,

The REPORT of RICHARD PETERS, ISAAC NORRIS, and BENJAMIN FRANKLIN, Esquires, Commissioners appointed to treat with some Chiefs of the Ohio Indians, at Carlisle, in the County of Cumberland, by a Commission, bearing the Date the 22d Day of September, 1753.

May it please the GOVERNOR,

* * *

THE *Twightwees* and *Delawares* having had several of their great Men cut off by the *French* and their *Indians,* and all the Chiefs of the *Owendaets* being lately dead, it became necessary to condole their Loss; and no Business could be begun, agreeable to the *Indian* Customs, till the Condolences were passed; and as these could not be made, with the usual Ceremonies, for want of the Goods, which were not

The Oneida are one of the nations of the Iroquois Confederation. Scarrooyady's apparent preeminence in the Indian delegation is a sign of continuing Iroquois hegemony over the Ohio Indians, including the Delaware. Sometimes his name is translated Scarouady.

arrived, and it was uncertain when they would, the Commissioners were put to some Difficulties, and ordered the Interpreters to apply to *Scarrooyady*, an *Oneido* Chief, who had the Conduct of the Treaty in *Virginia*, and was a Person of great Weight in their Councils, and to ask his Opinion, whether the Condolences would be accepted by Belts and Strings, and Lists of the particular Goods intended to be given, with Assurances of their Delivery as soon as they should come. *Scarrooyady* was pleased with the Application; but frankly declared, that the *Indians* could not proceed to Business while the Blood remained on their Garments, and that the Condolences could not be accepted unless the Goods, intended to cover the Graves, were actually spread on the Ground before them. A Messenger was therefore forthwith sent to meet and hasten the Waggoners, since every Thing must stop till the Goods came.

* * *

The Forms of the Condolences, which depend entirely on *Indian* Custom, were settled in Conferences with *Scarrooyady*, and *Cayanguileguoa*, a sensible *Indian*, of the *Mohock* Nation, and a Person intimate with and much consulted by *Scarrooyady*, in which it was agreed to take the *Six Nations* along with us in these Condolences; and accordingly the proper Belts and Strings were made ready, and *Scarrooyady* prepared himself to express the Sentiments of both in the *Indian* Manner. And as the Goods arrived this Morning before the Break of Day, the several Sorts used on these Occasions were laid out; and the *Indians* were told that the Commissioners would speak to them at Eleven a Clock.

The Mohawk are the most pro-British of the nations of the Iroquois Confederation.

AT A MEETING OF THE COMMISSIONERS, AND INDIANS, AT CARLISLIE, THE FIRST DAY OF OCTOBER, 1753.

PRESENT,

Richard Peters, Isaac Norris, Benjamin Franklin,
Esquires, Commissioners.
The Deputies of the Six Nations, Delawares, Shawonese, Twightwees, and Owendaets.

Conrad Weiser,
Andrew Montour, Interpreters.

James Wright,
John Armstrong, Esquires, Members of the Assembly.

The Magistrates, and several other Gentlemen Freeholders of the County of *Cumberland*.

The Speech of the Commissioners.

Brethren, Six Nations, Delawares, Shawonese, Twightwees, and Owendaets,

THOUGH the City of *Philadelphia* be the Place where all *Indians* should go, who have Business to transact with this Government, yet at your Request * * * he has been pleased on this particular Occasion to dispense with your coming there, and has done us the Honour to depute us to receive and treat with you at this Town, in his Place and Stead; this is set forth in his Commission, which we now produce to you, under the Great Seal of this Province, the authentick Sign and Testimony of all Acts of Government.

Scarrooyady performs the critically important Condolence Ceremony for the Pennsylvanians.

Brethren,

BY this String we acquaint you, that the *Six Nations* do, at our Request, join with us in condoling the Losses you have of late sustained by the Deaths of several of your Chiefs and principal Men; and that *Scarrooyady* is to deliver for both what has been agreed to be said on this melancholy Occasion.

Here the Commissioners gave a String of Wampum.

Then Scarrooyady spoke as follows:

Brethren, the Twightwees *and* Shawonese,

IT has pleased Him who is above, that we shall meet here To-day, and see one another; I and my Brother *Onas* join together to speak to you. As we know that your Seats at Home are bloody, we wipe away the Blood, and set your Seats in Order at your Council Fire, that you may sit and consult again in Peace and Comfort as formerly; that you may hold the ancient Union, and strengthen it, and continue your old friendly Correspondence.

Here a String was given.

Brethren, Twightwees *and* Shawonese,

WE suppose that the Blood is now washed off. We jointly, with our Brother *Onas,* dig a Grave for your Warriors, killed in your Country; and we bury their Bones decently; wrapping them up in these Blankets; and with these we cover their Graves.

Here the Goods were given to the Twightwees and Shawonese.

Brethren, Twightwees *and* Shawonese,

I, and my Brother *Onas,* jointly condole with the Chiefs of your Towns, your Women and Children, for the Loss you have sustained. We partake of your Grief, and mix our Tears with yours. We wipe your Tears from your Eyes, that you may see the Sun, and that every Thing may become clear and pleasant to your Sight; and we desire you would mourn no more.

Here a Belt was given.

Mutatis mutandis is a Latin phrase meaning "by changing those things which need to be changed." In other words, essentially the same message was then relayed to the Delawares.

The same was said to the *Delawares, mutatis mutandis.*

AND then he spoke to the *Owendaets,* in these Words:

Our Children, and Brethren, the Owendaets,

YOU have heard what I and my Brother *Onas* have jointly said to the *Twightwees, Shawonese,* and *Delawares:* We have now come to speak to you. We are informed that your good old wise Men are all dead, and you have no more left.

WE must let you know, that there was a Friendship established by our and your Grandfathers; and a mutual Council Fire was kindled. In this Friendship all those then under the Ground, who had not yet obtained Eyes or Faces (that is, those unborn) were included; and it was then mutually promised to tell the same to their Children, and Childrens Children: But so many great Men of your Nation have died in so short a Time, that none but the Youths are left; and this makes us afraid, lest that Treaty, so solemnly established by your Ancestors, should be forgotten by you: We therefore now come to remind you of it, and renew it; we re-kindle the old Fire, and put on fresh Fuel.

Here a String was given.

THE other Speeches, of burying the Dead, *&c.* were the same as those to the *Twightwees,* &c:

AFTER each had been spoken to, *Scarrooyady* proceeded thus:

Brethren, Delawares, Shawonese, Twightwees, *and* Owendaets,

WE, the *English,* and *Six Nations,* do now exhort every one of you to do your utmost to preserve this Union and Friendship, which has so long and happily continued among us: Let us keep the Chain from rusting, and prevent every Thing that may hurt or break it, from what Quarter soever it may come.

THEN the Goods allotted for each Nation, as a Present of Condolence, were taken away by each, and the Council adjourn'd to the next day.

AT A MEETING OF THE COMMISSIONERS, AND INDIANS, AT CARLISLIE, THE 2D OF OCTOBER, 1753.

The SPEECH of the Commissioners.

Following the condolences, the Pennsylvanians promise the Indians gifts.

B*rethren,* Six Nations, Delawares, Shawonese, Twightwees, *and* Owendaets

NOW that your Hearts are eased of their Grief, and we behold one another with cheerful Countenances, we let you know that the Governor, and good People of *Pennsylvania,* did not send us to receive you empty-handed; but put something into our Pockets, to be given to such as should favour us with friendly Visit: These Goods we therefore request you would accept of, and divide amongst all that are of your Company, in such Proportions as shall be agreeable to you. You know how to do this better than we. What we principally desire, is, that you will consider this Present as a Token of our cordial Esteem for you; and use it with a Frugality becoming your Circumstances, which call at this Time for more than ordinary Care.

Brethren,

WITH Pleasure we behold here the Deputies of five different Nations, *viz.* the *United Six Nations,* the *Delawares,* the *Shawonese,* the *Twightwees,* and the *Owendaets.* Be pleased to cast your Eyes towards this Belt, whereon six Figures are delineated, holding one another by the Hands. This is a just Resemblance of our present Union: The five first Figures representing the five Nations, to which you belong, as the sixth does the Government of *Pennsylvania*; with whom you are linked in a close and firm Union. In whatever Part the Belt is broke, all the Wampum runs off, and render the Whole of no Strength or Consistency. In like Matter, should you break Faith with one another, or with this Government, the Union is dissolved. We would therefore hereby place before you the Necessity of preserving your Faith entire to one another, as well as to this Government. Do not separate: Do not part on any Score. Let no Differences nor Jealousies subsist a Moment between Nation and Nation; but join all together as one Man, sincerely and heartily. We on our Part shall always perform our Engagements to every one of you. In Testimony whereof, we present you with this Belt.

They also provide a nice wampum belt signifying alliance.

Here the Belt was given.

* * *

Scarrooyady, Speaker.

Brother Onas,

WHAT we have now to say, I am going to speak, in Behalf of the *Twightwees, Shawonese, Delawares,* and *Owendaets.*

YOU have, like a true and affectionate Brother, comforted us in our Affliction. You have wiped away the Blood from our Seats, and set them again in order. You have wrapped up the Bones of our Warriors, and covered the Graves of our wise Men; and wiped the Tears from our Eyes, and the Eyes of our Women and Children: So that we now see the Sun, and all Things become pleasant to our Sight. We shall not fail to acquaint our several Nations with your Kindness. We shall take Care that it be always remembered by us; and believe it will be attended with suitable Returns of Love and Affection.

* * *

Brother Onas,

THE *Ontawas, Cheepaways,* and the *French,* have struck us.—The Stroke was heavy, and hard to be borne, for thereby we lost our King, and several of our Warriors; but the Loss our Brethren, the *English,* suffered, we grieve for most. The Love we have had for the *English,* from our first Knowledge of them, still continues

Satisfied with the condolences and the promises of gifts, one of the Twightwee begins describing the recent French attack on his people. He spins this into reciprocal condolences for the British.

in our Breasts; and we shall ever retain the same ardent Affection for them.—We cover the Graves of the *English* with this Beaver Blanket. We mourn for them more than for our own People.

Here he spread on the Floor some Beaver Skins, sewed together in the Form of a large Blanket.

Then Scarrooyady spoke as follows:

Brother Onas,

Scarrooyady then acknowledges receiving the wampum belt for the Indians, and promises to take it back to the Ohio Country.

I SPEAK now on Behalf of all the *Indians* present, in Answer to what you said when you gave us the Goods and Belt. What you have said to us Yesterday is very kind, and pleases us exceedingly. The Speech which accompanied the Belt, is particularly of great Moment. We will take the Belt home to *Ohio,* where there is a greater and wiser Council than us, and consider it, and return you a full Answer. We return you Thanks for the Present.

Gave a String.

Brother Onas,

Scarrooyady puts pleasantness aside as he lays out his theories about why the French have invaded the "Lands over the Allegheny Hills," or Ohio Country. He blames the territorial ambitions of Pennsylvania and Virginia. His solution is simple: the British should leave and they should stay away.

LAST Spring, when you heard of the March of the *French* Army, you were so good as to send us Word, that we might be on our Guard: We thank you for this friendly Notice.

* * *

Brother Onas,

I DESIRE you would hear and take Notice of what I am about to say now. The Governor of *Virginia* desired Leave to build a strong House on *Ohio,* which came to the Ears of the Governor of *Canada*; and we suppose this caused him to invade our Country. We do not know his Intent; because he speaks with two Tongues. So soon we know his Heart, we shall be able to know what to do; and shall speak accordingly to him. We desire that *Pennsylvania* and *Virginia* would at present forbear settling on our Lands, over the *Allegheny* Hills. We advise you rather to call your People back on this Side the Hills, lest Damage should be done, and you think ill of us. Let none of your People settle beyond where they are now; nor on the *Juniata* Lands, till the Affair is settled between us and the *French*. We desire a Commission may be given to a Person intrusted by the Government of *Pennsylvania*; and that he may be directed to warn People from settling the *Indians* Lands, and impowered to remove them.

The Juniata River is a western tributary of the Susquehanna, the valley of which is in the area Pennsylvania claims as a result of the Albany Purchase of 1754.

Gave a Belt and String.

Brother Onas,

ALL we who are here desire you will hear what we are going to say, and regard it as a Matter of Moment: The *French* look on the great Number of your Traders at

Ohio with Envy; they fear they shall lose their Trade. You have more Traders than are necessary; and they spread themselves over our wide Country, at such great Distances, that we cannot see them, or protect them. We desire you will call back the great Number of your Traders, and let only three Sets of Traders remain; and order these to say in three Places, which we have appointed for their Residence, *viz. Logs-Town,* the Mouth of *Canawa,* and the Mouth of *Mohongely*; the *Indians* will then come to them, and buy their Goods in these Places, and no where else. We shall likewise look on them under our Care, and shall be accountable for them.

Scarrooyady went on to convey a number of complaints against English traders.

The locations identified by Scarrooyady are all convenient locations in the Ohio Country.

* * *

Gave a String.

Brother Onas,

The *English* Goods are sold at too dear a Rate to us. If only honest and sober Men were to deal with us, we think they might afford the Goods cheaper: We desire therefore, that you will take effectual Care hereafter, that none but such be suffered to come out to trade with us.

Gave a String.

Brother Onas,

Your Traders now bring scarce any Thing but Rum and Flour: They bring little Powder and Lead, or other valuable Goods. The Rum ruins us. We beg you would prevent its coming in such Quantities, by regulating the Traders. We never understood the Trade was to be for Whiskey and Flour. We desire it may be forbidden, and none sold in the *Indian* Country; but that if the *Indians* will have any, they may go among the Inhabitants, and deal with them for it. When these Whiskey Traders come, they bring thirty or forty Cags, and put them down before us, and make us drink; and get all the Skins that should go to pay the Debts we have contracted for goods bought of the Fair Traders; and by this Means, we not only ruin ourselves, but them too. These wicked Whiskey Sellers, when they have once got the *Indians* in Liquor, make them sell their very Clothes from their Backs.—In short, if this Practice be continued, we must be inevitably ruined: We most earnestly therefore beseech you to remedy it.

A treble String.

* * *

Brother Onas,

Before I finish, I must tell you, we all earnestly request you will please to lay all our present Transactions before the Council of *Onondago,* that they may know we do nothing in the Dark. They may perhaps think of us, as if we did not know what we

Scarrooyady closes with a request to keep the Iroquois Grand Council at Onondaga informed.

were doing; or wanted to conceal from them what we do with our Brethren; but it is otherwise; and therefore make them acquainted with all our Proceedings.

* * *

Brother Onas,

I FORGOT something which I must now say to you; it is to desire you would assist us with some Horses to carry our Goods; because you have given us more than we can carry ourselves. Our Women and young People present you with this Bundle of Skins, desiring some Spirits to make them cheerful in their own Country; not to drink here.

Presented a Bundle of Skins.

* * *

Then the Indians withdrew.

* * *

AT A MEETING OF THE COMMISSIONERS, AND INDIANS, THE 4TH OF OCTOBER, 1753.

he Commissioners, unwilling to lose any Time, prepared their Answers early this Morning, and sent for the Indians; who having seated themselves, the following Speech was made to them:

Brethren, Six Nations, Delawares, Shawonese, Twightwees, *and* Owendaets,

THE several Matters delivered by you Yesterday have been well considered; and we are now going to return you our Answers.

* * *

Professing their lack of authority to fulfill any of the Indian requests, the commissioners promised to take a true account back to the lieutenant governor.

Brethren,

THE several Articles which contain your Observations on the *Indian* Traders, and the loose straggling Manner in which that Trade is carried on, thro' Countries lying at great Distances from your Towns—Your Proposals to remedy this, by having named three Places for the Traders to reside in, under your Care and Protection, with a Request, that the Province would appoint the particular Persons to be concerned in this Trade, for whom they will be answerable—What you say about the vast Quantities of Rum, and its ill Effects, and that no more may be brought amongst you; all these have made a very strong Impression upon our Minds; and was it now in our Power to rectify these Disorders, and to put Matters on the Footing you propose, we would do it with great Pleasure: But these are Affairs which more immediately concern the Government; in these therefore, we shall imitate your Example, by laying them before the Governor, assuring you, that our heartiest Representations of the Necessity of these

Regulations shall not be wanting, being convinced, that unless something effectual be speedily done in these Matters, the good People of this Province can no longer expect Safety or Profit in their Commerce, nor the Continuance of your Affection.

Brethren,

WE will send an Account to *Onondago* of all that has been transacted between us.

WE will assist you with Horses for the Carriage of the Goods given you.

WE grant your Women and young Men their Request for Rum, on Condition it be not delivered to them until you shall have passed the Mountains.

* * *

Brethren, Six Nations, Delawares, Shawonese, Twightwees, *and* Owendaets,

WE have something to say to you, to which we entreat you will give your closest Attention, since it concerns both us and you very much.

Brethren,

WE have held a Council on the present Situation of your Affairs. We have Reason to think, from the Advices of *Taaf* and *Callender,* that it would be too great a Risque, considering the present Disorder Things are in at *Ohio,* to increase the Quantity of Goods already given you: We therefore acquaint you, that, though the Governor has furnished us with a larger Present of Goods, to put into your publick Store-house, as a general Stock, for your Support and Service, and we did intend to have sent them along with you; we have, on this late disagreeable Piece of News, altered our Minds, and determined, that the Goods shall not be delivered till the Governor be made acquainted with your present Circumstances, and shall give his own Orders for the Disposal of them. And that they may lie ready for your Use, to be applied for, whenever the Delivery may be safe, seasonable, and likely to do you the most Service; we have committed them to the Care of your good Friend *George Croghan,* who is to transmit to the Governor, by Express, a true and faithful Account how your Matters are likely to turn out; and on the Governor's Order, and not otherwise, to put you into the Possession of them.

The attending Indians came away with little but hollow promises. No action was taken to regulate trade or settlement. Furthermore, the commissioners put their £800 worth of gifts into the hands of George Croghan, an Indian trader, rather than simply conveying them to the Indians as was customary.

THIS we hope you will think a prudent Caution, and a Testimony of our Care for your real Good and Welfare.

* * *

AFTER this Difficulty was got over, nothing else remained to be done; and as the Absence of these *Indians* was dangerous, the Commissioners put an End to the Treaty, and took their Leave of them, making private Presents at parting, to such of the Chiefs, and others, as were recommended by the Interpreters to their particular Notice.

THUS, may it please the Governor, we have given a full and just Account of all our Proceedings, and we hope our Conduct will meet with his Approbation. But, in Justice to these *Indians,* and the Promises we made them, we cannot close our Report, without taking Notice, That the Quantities of strong Liquors sold to

Despite their professed inability to take action, the commissioners do appear to be sincere. They appended a plea to the governor to the end of their report.

these *Indians* in the Places of their Residence, and during their Hunting Seasons, from all Parts of the Counties over *Sasquehannah,* have increased of late to an inconceivable Degree, so as to keep these poor *Indians* continually under the Force of Liquor, that they are hereby become dissolute, enfeebled and indolent when sober, and untractable and mischievous in their Liquor, always quarrelling, and often murdering one another: That the Traders are under no Bonds, nor give any Security for their Observance of the Laws, and their good Behaviour; and by their own Intemperance, unfair Dealings, and Irregularities, will, it is to be feared, entirely estrange the Affections of the *Indians* from the *English*; deprive them of their natural Strength and Activity, and oblige them either to abandon their Country, or submit to any Terms, be they ever so unreasonable, we shall stand excused in recommending in the most earnest Manner, the deplorable State of these *Indians,* and the heavy Discouragements under which our Commerce with them at present labours to the Governor's most serious Consideration, that some good and speedy Remedies may be provided before it be too late.

November 1, 1753.
RICHARD PETERS,
ISAAC NORRIS,
BENJ. FRANKLIN.

SUPPLEMENTAL DOCUMENTS

JOHN HECKWELDER

The Coming of Miquon

John Heckwelder, a Moravian missionary, related a Delaware story about the first encounter between Mohegans and Europeans. They met the Dutch (whom they call the Miquon) somewhere on the Hudson River estuary. Alcohol and cross-cultural confusion played a significant role in the interactions of these peoples from the outset.

SOURCE: John Heckwelder, "The Coming of Miquon," in *Traditions of the North American Indians,* James Athearn Jones, ed., vol. 2 (London: Henry Colburn and Richard Bentley, 1830), pp. 99–105.

* * *

A great many seasons ago, when men with a white skin had never been seen in the land of the Mohegans, before the Fire-eater had come to take the place of the Yagesho, or the pale-face had succeeded to the less destructive Mammoth; some men of our nation, who were out at a place where the sea widens, espied, far away on the bosom of the Great Lake, a very large creature floating on the water. It was such an object as they had never seen before. Fear of this creature immediately filling their bosoms, they hastily returned to the shore. Having apprised their countrymen of what they had seen, they pressed them to accompany them, and make further discoveries of its nature and its purpose in coming thither. Launching their canoes, they hurried out together, and saw with increased astonishment the wonderful object which was approaching. Their conjectures were very various as to what it was; some believed it to be a great fish, or animal; while others were of the opinion that it was a very big house floating on the bosom of the Great Lake. They were not long in concluding that this wonderful and mysterious object was moving towards the land, and they also saw that it was endued with life.

Deeming it proper to inform all their brethren, to whom intelligence could be conveyed, of what was coming, that they might be on their guard, they dispatched swift runners and fast rowers in every direction, to the east, west, and north, to carry the news to the scattered chiefs and tribes, that they might gather their warriors together, and prepare to combat, if need were, the strange creature. Soon, the chiefs and warriors of the neighboring tribes were collected in great numbers at that part of the shore which the strange creature was clearly approaching. It soon came so near that they were able to make it out to be a large moving house, in which, as they supposed, the Great Spirit himself was present, and coming to visit them.

Wishing to receive him in a manner which should make their sense of his goodness to them and their fathers, to the giver of the corn, and the meat, and the victory over their enemies, they deliberated in what manner that object could be best accomplished. The first thing was to provide plenty of meat for a sacrifice, and with this in view the best hunters were dispatched to the forest, in quest of those animals supposed to be most acceptable to the mighty guest. The women were directed to prepare the *tasmanane* and pottage in the best manner. All the idols were brought out, examined, and put in order. As a grand dance was always supposed to be an agreeable entertainment to the Great Spirit, one was ordered, not only for his gratification, but that it might, with the aid of a sacrifice, appease him, if he were angry with them, and induce him to stay his hand, rather than slay them.

The priests and *powwows* were called, and set to work to determine, if possible, what this remarkable event portended, and what the possible result might be. They came habited in their robes of magic, skins of black bears, the head, nose, ears, teeth, as also the legs, with the long claws, appearing the same as when the animal lived, with a huge pair of buffalo-horns upon the head, and a large bushy tail projecting from behind. Some were frightfully painted, some had the skin of an owl drawn over their heads, and some had snakes wreathed around their bodies. To them, and to the chiefs and wise men of the nation, the women and children, and the men of inferior note, were looking up for protection and advice. And now, filling up their gourds with water from the stump of a fallen cypress, they begin the work of incantation, by muttering over the magic water a charm that had hitherto been of potent influence, and words that called upon many spirits to assist in effecting the wishes of the masters of the spell. The spirits answered not, and the priests became so distracted with fears at the unusual deafness of those who had given them their power, that they increased the fever of apprehension they should have assisted to calm. The gourds, with the charmed water, fell from their hands, and although the dance was commenced with fervor and enthusiasm, yet, such was the alarm, that it did not possess the regularity and order with which the Great Spirit through songs, dances, and sacrifices, must be approached.

While in this situation, those men in canoes who had approached nearest to the strange object returned, and declared that it was a great house painted of various colors, and crowded with human beings. They thought it certain that it was the Great Spirit, bringing them some gift which they did not possess before. Other messengers soon arrived, who had seen the inhabitants of the house, and made a report which did not lessen their wonder, fear, or curiosity. They told their friends that they were men of a different color from the Indians, and differently dressed; they were as white as the flesh of a plucked bird, and wore no skins; and one of them, who must be the Great Spirit himself, was dressed entirely in red. The great house, or whatever it was, continued to approach. While approaching, some one in it cried to them in a loud voice, and in a language which they could not understand, yet they shouted in reply, according to the custom of the Mohegans. Much frightened at the strange voices, and at the still stranger creature which floated towards them, many proposed to retreat to the hills for security; others opposed this, lest offence should be given their visitor, who would find them out and destroy them. At last, the great creature, which they now found to be a great canoe, stopped and at once the robes white as snow, which were spread over its numerous arms, fluttered in the winds like clouds in the season of ripe corn. Soon there were many of the strange men employed in gathering these robes into folds, as Indians pack skins.

Presently a canoe of smaller size approached the shore where the Indians sat, having in it the man who was dressed in red and many others. When he had landed, leaving his canoe with some of his men to guard it, he approached the Mohegan chiefs and warriors who were assembled in council, and had seated themselves in a circle, as is their custom when about to receive ambassadors and messengers of peace. The man in red walked fearlessly into the midst of them, and saluted them all with great kindness, taking a hand of each, which he shook very hard. The Indians, on their part, testified their gladness, and their friendship, and their emotions of joy and satisfaction at their arrival, by loud shots, and by rubbing their cheeks against those of their new acquaintances, and by patting them on the back.

Lost in admiration of the strangers, of their dress, so gay and dissimilar to that of the Indians, their manners so unlike, their features so different, and their language so unknown, the Mohegans could do nothing but wonder and applaud. A large portion of their admiration, was however, reserved for the man who wore the glittering red coat, and who, they doubted not, was the Great Spirit. The curiosity of the people was expressed in a thousand different ways; the priests wondered whether the Great Spirit knew and recognized them as old acquaintances; the warriors, whether the men who accompanied him were fleet, and courageous as themselves; and the women were very curious to know if the men were like our own men, and loudly expressed their determination to ascertain the fact. All agreed in this, that whether beings of this world, or of the world of dreams, they must be treated with great kindness, and fed upon the choicest viands of the tribe.

Meanwhile; a large hackhack, or gourd, was brought to the man in red by one of his servants, from which he poured an unknown liquor resembling rainwater, into a small clear cup of such an appearance as the Indians had never before seen. He drank the liquor from this cup, and filling it again, he handed it to the Mohegan chief standing next to him. The chief received it, smelt to it, and passed it untasted to the chief standing by him, who did the same, till it had been handled and smelt by all the Indians in the circle, while not one had tasted it. The man who took the cup was upon returning it to the supposed Manitou in red; when the Bender of the Pine Bow, one of the bravest Mohegans and stoutest warriors in the nation, rose and spoke to his brothers thus:

A manito, or manitou, is a spirit.

> It is not right for us to return the cup with its contents untasted. It is handed to us by the Manitou, that we may drink as he has done. To follow his example will be pleasing to him; it will show our confidence in him, and the courage which we have been told is highly valued by him. To return the cup with its contents untasted, will give him reason to think that we believe it to be the juice of the poison-tree; it will provoke his anger and bring destruction upon us all. It is for the good of the nation that the contents of the cup should be swallowed, and, as no one else will do it, the Bender of the Pine Bow devotes himself to the killing draught. It is better that one man should perish than that a whole nation should be destroyed.

The Bender of the Pine Bow then took the glass, and giving many directions, and bidding a solemn farewell to his family and friends, resolutely drank its fearful contents. Every eye was fixed upon the brave man, to see what effect the stranger liquor would produce. Soon he began to stagger, to whine fearfully, to roll up the white of his eyes, to shout, and to act a thousand other extravagancies. At last, he fell prostrate on the ground. His companions, supposing him dead, fell to bemoaning his fate, and his wife set up the death-howl; all thought him a martyr to his valor and his love for his nation. But the man in red only laughed at their grief, and by signs gave them to understand that he would rise again. He told them true; the chief awoke and declared to his friends that he had enjoyed, while apparently lifeless, the most delicious sensations, and that he had never before felt so happy as after he had drunk the cup. He asked the man in red for more; his wish was granted; the other people made the same request, and so was theirs; the whole assembly tasted the contents of the cup, and all became as mad and intoxicated as their leader. Soon was the Mohegan camp a scene of noise and tumult, brawl and bloodshed.

After the general madness had ceased, the man in red and his associates, who, while it lasted, had confined themselves to their canoe, returned to shore, and distributed presents, such as beads and axes, among the Indians. The two nations soon became familiar with each other, and a conversation ensued, wherein the wants and wishes of each, as far as they could be made intelligible, were conveyed by signs. The strangers gave them to understand that they must recross the Great Salt Lake, to the vales which contained their wives and little ones; but that they would be back again when the season of snows should have passed, and would bring with them more and richer presents. With these promises, they departed.

When the season of flowers came round again, it brought with it the man in red, and a great band of followers. The Indians were very glad to see the pale faces, who appeared equally pleased at the meeting. But the latter were much diverted, and made a great laugh at the uses to which the Indians had put their presents, for they had suspended the axes and hoes around their necks, and used the stockings for tobacco-pouches. The visitors now taught them the proper use of those implements. Having put handles to the axes and hoes, with the former they felled great trees, making the forest ring with their blows; with the latter they cut up the weeds which choked the maize. The various benefits conferred upon the Indians by their visitors confirmed them in the belief that they were indeed spiritual beings, he in the red being in their estimation the Supreme Manitou, and his attendants, the inferior Manitous. The visitors did not this time all go back in the canoes; many of them continued to abide with the Indians, who gave or sold them land, and lived very contentedly with them until they wished to dispossess them of the very grounds where they had buried the bones of their fathers. Wars were then commenced, and the Indians were soon dispossessed of the soil which was theirs by birthright.

DAVID ZEISBERGER

Delawares and the Allegheny River Valley

David Zeisberger, a Moravian missionary to the Delaware, related this account of the Delaware claim to the Allegheny River valley. In addition to establishing a territorial claim, the story presents the Iroquois as equals and insists that they recognized Delaware control over this land. Because this area includes the lands that Pennsylvania claims as a result of the Albany Purchase of 1754 (which transferred the territory from the Iroquois to Pennsylvania without the consent of the Delaware), Delaware insistence on the authority of this story may complicate matters. However, because the story is set around 1700, it remains unclear if the status of the land or the relationships between the three parties involved—Delaware, Pennsylvania, and Iroquois—changed in some important ways during the fifty years that followed. Zeisberger probably first heard this story in the 1770s.

SOURCE: David Zeisberger, *David Zeisberger's History of the Northern American Indians,* A. B. Hulbert and W. N. Schwarze, eds. (Ohio State Archaeological and Historical Society, 1910), pp. 32–33.

I must yet in passing notice how it came about that the Delawares, who had lived near the sea and along the Delaware River, came to Alleghene, where they were strangers and had no claim to the land. Some eighty years ago, more or less [1700], the whites being already in the country and many of the Delawares having moved far up the Delaware River, a party of these Indians, with the cousin of a chief as captain, went on a hunt. They were attacked by Cherokees, at that time dwelling along the Allegheny and its branches, and some of them were killed, the captain, a cousin of the chief, among the rest. The survivors fled to their homes, related to the chief what had happened and suggested that he give them more men in order that they might avenge themselves on their enemies. The chief, however, put them off and did not let them go, even though he sorrowed over the loss they had suffered.

After the lapse of a year the chief sent out several hundred men to avenge themselves of the Cherokees (the Delawares at that time already having European arms). When they arrived at the enemies' first towns along the Allegheny, they found no one, for all had fled at the news of the Delawares' approach. The latter pursued, the Cherokees constantly retreating until they were overtaken at the

Fort Duquesne occupies the future site of Pittsburgh.

great island at the fork where Pittsburg is now situated. Perceiving that the Delawares were strong in numbers, they had no heart to fight, though they stood ready with bow and arrow in hand; instead, their chiefs called to the Delawares to rest their arms and not fight. Afterwards they had an interview with the Delawares and surrendered themselves as prisoners. About half of them, however, dissatisfied with the capitulation, refused to surrender and escaped during the night, going down the river to the mouth of another river, now named the Cherokee River, where they landed and afterward settled along this stream, in the region in which they still live.

After the Delawares had finished with the Cherokees, the Six Nations [the Iroquois] arrived, having heard of the expedition of the Delawares. When they realized that the Delawares were masters of the situation, they professed satisfaction and said that they had come to assist them, but recognized that their aid was not now needed. Thereupon the Delawares gave them some of their prisoners as a present for their trouble and suffered them to go to their homes. Then the Delawares remained a long time at the Beaver Creek, to which they gave its name, in view of the animals that there abounded.

After that the Delawares turned their faces homeward but soon returned, and since that time this region has been inhabited by Delawares and year by year more have come. Later the Wiondates [Wynadots], in connection with a solemn council, recognized the claim they made to the territory, inasmuch as they had conquered it.

All this land and region, stretching as far as the creeks and waters that flow into the Alleghne the Delawares call Alligewinenk, which means, "a land into which they came from distant parts." The river itself, however, is called Alligewi Sipo. The whites have made Alleghene out of this, the Six Nations calling the river the Ohio.

With the Delawares the Six Nations carried on long wars before the coming of the white man, and even after the advent of the pale-face, but the former were always too powerful for the Six Nations. The latter were convinced that if they continued the wars, their total extirpation would be inevitable. The Six Nations indeed boast that they had overcome the Delawares but these will not grant it, stating that as the Six Nations recognized the superior strength of the Delawares they thought of a means of saving their honor and making peace so that it might not seem that they had been conquered by the Delawares.

Zeisberger then relates his take on the Delaware status as "women."

Soon after Pennsylvania had been settled by the whites. The Six Nations sent an embassy to the Delawares, opened negotiations and said: It is not profitable that all the nations should be at war with each other, for this would at length ruin the whole Indian race. They had, therefore, contrived a remedy by which this evil might be prevented while there was yet opportunity to do so. One nation should be the woman. She should be placed in the midst, while the other nations, who make war, should be the man and live around the woman. No one should touch or hurt the woman, and if any one did so, they would immediately say to him, "Why do you beat the woman?" Then all the men should fall upon him who has beaten her. The woman should not go to war but endeavor to keep the peace with all. Therefore, if the men that surround her should beat each other and the war be carried on with violence, the woman should have the right of addressing them, "Ye men, what are ye about; why do ye beat each other? We are almost afraid. Consider that your wives and children must perish unless you desist. Do you mean to destroy yourselves from the face of the earth?" The men should then hear and obey the woman. Ever since then the Six Nations have called the Delawares their cousins, i.e., their sister's children, and declared them to be the woman, dressed them in a woman's long habit, reaching down to the feet, though Indian women wear only short garments that reach but little below the knee, and fastened this about their bodies with a great, large belt of wampum. They adorned them with ear-rings, such as their women were accustomed to wear. Further, they hung a calabash filled with oil and beson [medicine] on their arms, therewith to anoint themselves and other nations. They also gave them a corn-pestle and a hoe. Each of these points was confirmed by delivering a belt of wampum and the whole ceremony observed with the greatest solemnity. One must not, however, think they actually dressed them in women's garments and placed a corn-pestle and hoe in their hands. It is to be understood in the same way as when the chiefs among the Indians lay out a trail several hundred miles through the woods, they cut away thorn and thicket, clear trees, rocks, and stones out of the way, cut through the hills, level up the track and strew it with white sand, so that they may easily go from one nation to another; but when one goes the way that has thus been cleared it is found to be full of wood and rocks and stones and all overgrown with thorns and thicket. The woman's garment signified that they should not engage in war, for the Delawares were great and brave warriors, feared by the other nations; the corn-pestle and hoe that they should engage in agriculture. The calabash with oil was to be used to cleanse the ears of the other nations, that they might attend to good and not to evil counsel. With the medicine or beson they were to heal those who were walking in foolish ways that they might come to their senses and incline their hearts to peace.

The Delaware nation is thus looked to for the preservation of peace and entrusted with the charge of the great belt of peace and the chain of friendship which they must take care to preserve inviolate and which they bear on their shoulders at its middle, the other nations and the Europeans holding the ends.

Thus it was brought about that the Delawares should be the cousins of the Six Nations and were made by them to be the women. Such a state of things was preserved until 1755, when a war broke out between the Indians and the white people into which the Delawares were enticed by the Six Nations.

* * *

JOHN WOOLMAN

Epistle from the Society of Friends, 1755

John Woolman (1720–1772) worked as a farmer, tailor, and schoolmaster. His journal, a celebrated spiritual autobiography, was first published in 1773. Within, he "took the traditional forms of Quaker journal writing and thrust into them his passionate response to evil and great inward turmoil over compromise."[1]

Well before this publication, Woolman became well known in Pennsylvania for his frustration with Quakers who placed their trust in the instruments of state rather than the power of God.

In 1755 the Pennsylvania Assembly's move toward levying a tax to support military efforts against frontier raids by the French and hostile Indians inspired Woolman and other purists like Israel Pemberton Jr. to challenge defense Quakers, who were willing to equivocate with the peaceable testimony. First, Woolman and twenty other prominent Quakers issued a declaration encouraging Quaker assemblymen to resign and advocating resistance to Pennsylvania's "war tax." These positions cut against traditional Quaker practice, which followed the apostle Paul's advice to be subject to the governing authorities, but they found many supporters among the Friends.

The following epistle encapsulates the theological argument behind the purist position. It was issued after the 1755 yearly meeting of the Philadelphia Friends. It lays out Woolman's confidence in divine power and his concern that resorting to worldly statecraft and war would undermine the spread of the peaceable kingdom.[2]

SOURCE: John Woolman, "Epistle from the Society of Friends," in *The Journal and Essays of John Woolman* (New York: Macmillan, 1922), p. 177.

To Friends on the continent of America.

Dear Friends

In an humble sense of Divine Goodness, & the gracious continuation of God's love to his people, we tenderly Salute you, and are at this time therein Engaged in mind, that all of us who profess the Truth as held for & published

---

1. Hugh Barbour and J. William Frost, *The Quakers* (New York: Greenwood, 1988), 119.

2. Barbour and Frost, *The Quakers* pp. 125–26.

by our worthy predecessors in this latter age of the world, may keep near to that Life which is the Light of men, & be strenghened to hold fast the profession of our Faith without wavering. That our trust may not be in man, but in the Lord alone, Who Ruleth in the Army of Heaven, and in the Kingdom of men, before whom the Earth is as the dust of the balance, and her Inhabitants as grasshoppers. Isa. xl. 22.

We (being convinced that the gracious design of the Almighty in sending his Son into the world, was to repair the breach made by Disobedience, to finish sin & transgression, that his Kingdom might come, and his will be done on Earth as it is in Heaven) have found it to be our duty to cease from those National Contests productive of Misery & bloodshed, and submit our cause to Him the Most High, whose tender Love to his Children exceeds the most warm Affections of Natural Parents, and who hath promised to his Seed throughout the Earth, as to one individual, "I will never leave thee, nor forsake thee." Heb. xiii. 5.

And as we, through the Gracious dealings of the Lord our God, have had Experience of that work which is carried on, "not by Earthly might, nor by power, but by my spirit , saith the Lord of Hosts," Zech. iv. 6; By which operation that Spiritual Kingdom is set up which is to subdue and break in pieces all Kingdoms that oppose it, and shall stand for ever. In a deep sense thereof, and of the safety, Stability and peace there is in it, we are desirous that all who profess the Truth may be inwardly acquainted with it and thereby be qualified to conduct in all parts of our life as becomes our peaceable profession. And we trust, as there is a faithfull continuance to depend wholly upon the almighty Arm from one generation to another the peacable kingdom will gradually be extended from Sea to Sea, and from the river to the ends of the earth," Zech. ix. 10; to the completion of those profesies already begun, that Nation shall not lift up Sword against nation nor learn war any more. Isa. ii. 4. Micah. iv. 3.

And, dearly beloved Friends, seeing we have these promises, and believe that God is beginning to fulfil them, let us constantly endeavour to have our minds sufficiently disentangled from the surfeiting cares of this life and redeemed from the Love of the world that no earthly possessions nor Enjoyments may byas our judgments or turn us from that resignation, and entire trust in God, to which his blessing is most surely annexed: then may we say, Our Redeemer is Mighty, he will plead our cause for us. Jer. 1. 34. And if for the further promoting his most gracious purposes in the Earth he should give us to taiste of that bitter cup which his faithfull ones have often partook of, O that we may be rightly prepared to receive it!

And now, dear Friends, with respect to the Commotions and Stirrings of the powers of the earth at this time near us, we are desirous that none of us may be moved thereat; "but repose ourselves in the munition of that rock that all these shakings shall not move, even in the knowledge and feeling of the Eternal power of God, keeping us Subjectly given up to his Heavenly Will and feel it daily to mortify that which remains in any of us which is of this world for the worldly part in any is the changeable part, and that is up and down, full and empty, joyfull and sorrowfull, as things go well or ill in this world. for as the Truth is but one and many are made partakers of its spirit, so the world is but one and many are made partakers of the Spirit of it: & so many as do partake of it, so many will be straitened and perplexed with it. But they who are "single to the Truth, waiting daily to feel the life and Virtue of it in their hearts, these shall rejoice in the midst of Adversity."[3] and have to experience with the profet, that though the fig-tree shall not blossom neither shall fruit be in the vines, The labour of the Olive shall fail, & the fields shall yield no meat; the flock shall be cut off from the fold and there shall be no herd in the stall yet with they rejoyce in the Lord and Joy in the God of their Salvation." Hab. iii. 17, 18.

If contrary to this we profess the Truth & not living under the power and influence of it, are producing fruits disagreeable to the purity thereof, and trust to the strength of man to Suport ourselves therein, our confidence will be vain, for He, who removed the Hedge from his vinyard, and gave it to be trodden under foot by reason of the wild grapes it produced remains unchangible: and if, for the chatisement of wickedness and the further promoting his own Glory He doth arise even to shake terribly the earth, who then may oppose him, & prosper!

We remain in the Love of the gospel your friends and brethren.
Signed in and on behalf of our said meeting, by

JACOB HOWELL,	JOHN EVANS,
JAMES BARTRAM,	MORDECAI YARNALL,
JOSEPH WHITE,	DANIEL STANTON,
JOHN SCARBOROUGH,	JOHN CHURCHMAN,
JOHN WOOLMAN,	WILLIAM MORRIS,
JOSIAH FOSTER,	ISAAC ANDREWS,
JOSEPH TOMLINSON,	SAMUEL ABBOTT.

WILLIAM SMITH

A Brief State of the Province of Pennsylvania, 1755

William Smith's pamphlet is a political hatchet job. Smith's patron was Thomas Penn, and his targets were the Quakers and to a lesser extent, the assembly and German immigrants. The pamphlet was first published in London in an attempt

3. From [Quaker writer] Stephen Crisp's epistle.

to influence Parliament and Crown officials. Smith presented himself as a native of Pennsylvania, although he spent only a short time in Philadelphia. He begins by explaining why, despite its wealth, Pennsylvania lacks a significant military.

SOURCE: William Smith, *A Brief State of the Province of Pennsylvania ...* (London: R. Griffiths, 1755), pp. 9–44.

Dear Sir,

In your last, you were pleased to desire some Account of the State of *Pennsylvania,* together with the Reasons why we, who are esteemed one of the richest Colonies in *North America,* are the most backward in contributing to the Defense of the *British* Dominions in these Parts, against the present unwarrantable Invasions of the *French.* As I have been many Years a Spectator, and think an impartial one, of the public Measures pursued in this Province, I shall very readily satisfy your whole Desire. We are now in an alarming Situation, but we have brought the Evil upon ourselves, and Things are now come to that Crisis, that if I was under no Obligation to satisfy your Expectations, yet I should deem my Silence an unpardonable Neglect of Duty I owe to my Country.—

You were rightly informed when you were told that of all the *British* Colonies in *North America, Pennsylvania* is the most flourishing. Its Staple is chiefly Provisions, of which it produces enough to maintain itself, and a Hundred thousand Men besides. From the Port of *Philadelphia,* at least 400 Sail of Vessels clear out annually. The Inhabitants are computed at about Two hundred and twenty thousand, of whom, it is thought near one half are *Germans.* Of the Residue not quite two Fifths are *Quakers.* Above that Number are *Presbyterians;* and the remaining Fifth are of the *establish'd Church,* with some few *Anabaptists.*

The Legislature is composed of a Governor and Assembly; but the Council makes no Part of it. The Assembly are chosen annually, and claim a Right, by Charter, to fit on their own Adjournment, without being prorogued or dissolved by their Governors, although the *Attorney-General* of *England*, and many other eminent Lawyers, have given their Opinion to the contrary. The Powers they enjoy are extraordinary, and some of them so repugnant, that they are the Source of the greatest Confusion in the Government. In order clearly to makes this out, we must look backward a considerable number of Years.

As the Colony was first settled chiefly by *Quakers*, the Powers of Government rested for the most Part in them; which they conducted with great Mildness and Prudence, not having as yet conceived any Thoughts of turning *Religion* into a *political Scheme for Power.*

A great many Circumstances concurred to fix them in the good Opinion of the World. The First of this Profession strove to recommend themselves by their strict Honesty, and were a sober, thoughtful People. The civil Constitution was then in its Infancy, and its Principles found. No great Art was required in the Administration of it, and no bad Effects were felt from the extraordinary Privileges granted to the People, for the more expeditious Settlement of the Colony.

* * *

Smith develops his idea that while republican forms of government are well suited to the early stages of political development they begin to fail as time passes. He also suggests that the Quakers of the present are quite different (and not in a good way) from those of the founding generation (that is, William Penn).

The Consequence of this is clear. The Government, instead of drawing nearer to the *mixt Forms*, as it ought in Proportion to its Growth, is now, in fact, more a *pure Republic*, than when there were not ten-thousand Souls in it. The Inconveniencies of this we now begin to feel severely, and they must continually increase with the Numbers of the People, till the Government becomes at last so unwieldy as to fall a Prey to any *Invader*, or sink beneath its own Weight, unless a speedy Remedy is applied.—

* * *

Unchecked, the republican tendencies of the Quakers dominated the assembly, which, in turn, eviscerated the power of the governor (a proprietary appointee) and took taxation and the payment of the lieutenant governor's salary and the ability to dispense patronage in the form of government jobs into its own hands. Consequently, the assembly refused to make meaningful contributions to the defense of the empire. Indeed, they failed to make much effort to defend their own western frontiers.

Possessed of such unrestrained Powers and Privileges, they seem quite intoxicated; are fractious, contentious, and disregard the Proprietors and their Governors. Nay, they seem even to claim a kind of Independency of their Mother-Country, despising the Orders of the Crown, and refusing to contribute their Quota, either to the general Defense of *America*, or that of their own particular Province.

As a glaring Instance of the former, I need only mention their Opposition to Governor *Thomas*, in raising Soldiers to send against the *Spaniards* in the *West-Indies*, and their absolute Refusal to contribute a Farthing for that Service. Since that Time, during the whole Course of the late War, they have often been called upon by the Crown, and by Governor *Shirley* of the *Massachusetts*, for the Expedition against *Cape-Breton*, &c. To all which, if they have at any Time contributed, it has been done indirectly, and in a Manner shameful to this rich Province; so grudgingly, and in such small Sums, as rather to hurt than serve the common Cause.

Forgetful of the public Good, they seem wholly to have employed themselves in grasping after Power, altho' it is plain they have already too much of this, and such as is really inconsistent and self-destructive.

Smith makes a reference to King George's War (1740–48), which corresponded to the War of the Austrian Succession. The expedition to Cape Breton was, despite the lack of support from Pennsylvania, amazingly successful.

Nor have they been more attentive to the Defense of their own particular Province, than of his Majesty's *American* Dominions, in general.

In *Pennsylvania*, we have but one small Fortification [Fort Augusta], and that raised and supported at the Expense of private People. The Proprietors, indeed, generously made us a Present of twelve large Cannon, part of the twenty-six we have mounted, and they have also given the Gunner of the Fort a Salary of twenty Pounds *per Annum* towards his Support. We are otherwise entirely naked, without Arms or Ammunition, and exposed to every Invasion, being under no Obligation to military Duty. In the last War, one of the *Spanish* Privateers came up the *Delaware,* within a few Miles of this City; and when those, who were not *Quakers,* took the Alarm, and associated themselves for the Defense of the Country, they not only received no Encouragement from the Assembly, but were abused and reproached for their Pains, and the *Dutch* or *Germans* kept back from joining in the Association, by all possible under-hand Practices.

The *French*, well apprized of this defenseless and disjointed State, and presuming on the religious Principles of our ruling People, have, the Year before last, invaded the Province, and have actually three Forts, now erected far within the Limits of it. Justly, therefore, may we presume that, as soon as War is declared, they will take Possession of the whole, since they may really be said to have stronger Footing in it than we, having three Forts in it supported at public Expense, and we but one small Fort, supported only by private Gentlemen.

This references a Virginian attempt to construct a fort at the Forks of the Ohio. After they occupied the site, the French built Fort Duquesne.

'Tis true our Neighbors, the *Virginians,* have taken the Alarm, and called on our Assistance to repel the common Enemy, knowing that if the *French* hold Footing in *Pennsylvania,* their Turn must be next. In like manner, the several Governors, and ours among the rest, have received his Majesty's gracious Orders to raise Money, and the armed Force of their respective Governments on such an Emergency; and had these Orders been complied with last Winter, the *French* would neither have been able to drive the *Virginians* from the Fort they begun in the back Parts of *Pennsylvania,* nor yet to get Possession of one third Part of the Province, which they now have undoubtedly got thro' the Stubbornness and Madness of our Assemblies.

* * *

But here two Questions will naturally arise.

1. Why are our Assemblies against defending a Country, in which their own Fortunes and Estates lie, if it is really in Danger?
2. Why have not the several Sums been accepted, which they have offered for the King's Use?

Smith then poses the question he wants to answer: Why has the assembly failed to defend itself against the French threat?

With regard to the first, it may seem a *Solecism* in Politics, for a People not to defend their own Property when it is actually *invaded,* unless they were certain of the Friendship of the *Invaders.*

I shall not, however, be so uncharitable as to suppose our political *Quakers* reckon it indifferent, whether, or not, the *French* shall make themselves Masters of this Province, notwithstanding Persons at a Distance may be apt to judge so for the following Reasons. 1*st,* From the continued Refusal of our Assemblies to defend the Province. 2*dly,* From the extraordinary Indulgence and Privileges granted to *Papists* in this Government:—Privileges plainly repugnant to all our political

Interests, considered as a Frontier-Colony, bordering on the *French,* and one half of the People an uncultivated Race of *Germans,* liable to be seduced by every enterprising Jesuit, having almost no Protestant Clergy among them to put them on their Guard, and warn them against Popery.

Tho' this might be insinuated, yet from Observation I have Reason to believe, that most of the *Quakers* without Doors are really against Defense from Conscience and their religious Tenets; but for those within Doors, I cannot but ascribe their Conduct rather to Interest than Conscience.

Our Assemblies apprehend, that as soon as they agree to give sufficient Sums for the regular Defense of the Country, it would strike at the Root of all their Power, as *Quakers,* by making a *Militia-Law* needful, in Time of Danger. Such a Law, they presume, would alter the whole Face of Affairs, by creating a vast Number of new Relations, Dependencies, and Subordinations in the Government. The *Militia,* they suppose, would all vote for Members of Assembly, and being dependent on their Officers, would probably be influenced by them. The Officers, again, as they imagine, would be influenced by the Government; and thus the *Quakers* fear they would soon be out-voted in most Places. For this Cause, they will suffer the Country to fall into the last Extremity, hoping that when it is so, our Neighbors will, for their own Sakes, defend it, without obliging them to pass a Law, which, they fear, would so soon strip them of their darling Power. But this Backwardness of theirs has quite a contrary effect; for the neighboring Colonies, seeing this Colony, that is immediately attacked, doing nothing, refuse to exert themselves for a People, who are able, but unwilling, to defend themselves.

Thus much in answer to the *first* Question.

With regard to the *second,* little need be said to shew why the Monies they have offered for the King's Service never could be accepted of. For while they have the foresaid Apprehensions from a Law for the Defense of the Country, it must be plainly repugnant to their Interest, ever to offer Money for this Purpose, unless in such a Manner as they know to be inconsistent with the Duty of a Governor to pass their Bill into a Law. This will be fully understood from what follows, which will also show by what Means they save Appearances among the People, without doing any Thing for the Public.

* * *

Smith then explains the conflicts between a series of governors and the assembly over defense appropriations.

Hence it is that this Province is reduced to the most miserable Condition—The People at Variance, and distrustful of each other! A *French* Enemy and their Savage Allies advance far into our Territory! The People on our Frontiers liable to be murdered or driven from their Habitations! Our Lives and all our sacred rights exposed an easy Prey!—And all this owing to the Infatuation and detestable Policy of a set of Men who mind no Consequences, provided they can secure their own Power and their Seats in Assembly.

A Petition from a Thousand of these poor Families, who inhabit the back Parts of the Colony; was presented to the Assembly last *August,* soon after *Washington's* Defeat, praying that they might be furnished with Arms and Ammunition for their Defence; but the petition was rejected with Scorn. Our *Indian* Allies have often desired us to build Forts, to which their Wives and Children might fly in time of Danger, and have just now sent down to the Governor, begging he would direct the Building a *Stockade,* or wooden Fort, in which they offer to defend themselves and us, from the Incursions of the Enemy; but the Assembly, to be consistent with themselves, and shew that they are religiously bent on the Ruin of their Country, refused to give any Money for this Purpose, and gave the *Indians* for Answer, that if they were afraid of the Enemy, they might retire further down, and come within the settled Parts of the Province.

Thus the noblest Opportunity was lost that could have been offered, or keeping our *Indians* steady, and for building a Fort at a small Expense, in a Pass so commodiously situated between the Mountains that it would have effectually covered and defended two of our Frontier Counties, from the Inroads of the *French* and their *Indians.*

From what has been said, it clearly appears how much we suffer by having all public Monies in such Hands. Were the Case otherwise, Matters might be managed with Secrecy, Ease, Expedition, Success, and a small Expense, by embracing the proper Opportunities. But these Opportunities, being once lost, are often never to be recalled, as is too well confirmed by the Settlements of the *French* at *Crown-Point* and on the *Ohio,* both which might have been prevented at first, with one fiftieth Part of the Expense it will now take to dislodge them, had not the Hands of all our Governors been tied up, by having the Disposal of no Monies on such Emergencies, nor any Hopes of obtaining it from our Assemblies, if they should advance any Sums for the public Service.

But here it may be justly asked, By what means the *Quakers,* who are so small a Part of the Inhabitants, and whose Measures are so unpopular, get continually chosen into our Assemblies?

Satisfied with his case against the Quakers, Smith goes on to ask, Why does this state of affairs persist? He then describes their alliance with German immigrants. His characterization of the Germans is xenophobic and inaccurate.

Before the late *Spanish* War, a considerable Number of our Assembly were of other Denominations; but at that Time being called upon by Governor *Thomas,* to arm for their own Defense, and the Annoyance of his Majesty's Enemies, they were alarmed with the Prospect of losing their Power, if they should comply, as was shown above; and therefore they entered into Cabals in their yearly Meeting, which is convened just before the Election, and being composed of Deputies from all the monthly Meetings in the Province, is the finest Scheme that could possibly be projected, for conducting political Intrigues, under the Mask of Religion. They likewise had Recourse to a *German* Printer, who was once one of the *French* Prophets in *Germany,* and is shrewdly suspected to be a *Popish* Emissary, who now prints a News-Paper entirely in the *German* Language, which is universally read and believed by the *Germans* in this Province. This Man, whose Name is *Saüer,* they took into their Pay, and by his Means have told the *Germans* there was a Design to enslave them; to force their young Men to be Soldiers, make them serve as Pioneers, and go down to work upon our Fortifications;—that a military Law was to be made, insupportable Taxes to be laid upon them, and in a Word, that all the Miseries they suffered in *Germany,* with heavy Aggravations would be their Lot, unless they joined to keep in the *Quakers*, under whose Administration they had so long enjoyed Ease and Tranquility; and to force out of the Assembly, all those who were like to join the Governor, in giving Money for annoying the Enemy.

In consequence of this, the *Germans,* who had hitherto continued peaceful, without meddling in Elections, came down in Shoals, and carried all before them. Near 1800 of them voted in the County of *Philadelphia,* which threw the Balance on the Side of the *Quakers*, tho' their Opponents, in that grand struggle, voted near 500 more than ever lost an Election before.

The *Quakers* having found out this Secret, have ever since excluded all other Persuasions from the Assembly, constantly calling in the *Germans* to their Aid, by means of this Printer.

But the keeping the *Quakers* in, is not the worst Consequence of these insidious Practices with the *Germans*. The bad Effects of it will probably be felt thro' many Generations.—The *Germans,* instead of being a peaceable industrious People as before, now finding themselves of such Consequence, are grown insolent, sullen, and turbulent; in some Counties threatening even the Lives of all who oppose their Views. The *Quakers,* in order to keep them from taking up Arms in Defense of the Province, or joining in Elections with their Opponents, have much alienated their Affections from the Government, by telling them there is a Design against their Liberties. They are taught to have but one and the same Idea for Government and Slavery. All who are not of their Party they call *Governors-Men,* in Derision. They give out that they are a Majority, and strong enough to make the Country their own; and indeed, as they are poured in upon us in such Numbers (upwards of 5000 being imported this last Year) I know nothing that will hinder them, either from soon being able to give us Law and Language, or else, by joining with the *French,* to eject all the *English* Inhabitants.

That this may be the Case, is too much to be feared, since, as I remarked already, they refused, almost to a Man, to bear Arms in the Time of the late War. They say it is all one to them which King gets the Country, since, if they remain quiet, they will be permitted to enjoy their Estates, under the Conqueror, whoever he is; and as they have, many of them, lived under *Popish* Rulers before in their own Country, they give out that they know the worst that can happen.

Smith then speculates about French plans.

And, indeed, it is clear that the *French* have turned their Hopes upon this great Body of *Germans*. They have now got Possession of the vast and exceeding fruitful Country upon the *Ohio*, just behind our *German* Settlements. They know our *Germans* are extremely ignorant, and think a large Farm the greatest Blessing in Life. Therefore, by sending their *Jesuitical* Emissaries among them, to persuade them over to the *Popish* Religion, they will draw them from the *English,* in Multitudes, or perhaps lead them in a Body against us. This is plainly a Scheme laid by the *French* many Years ago, and uniformly pursued till this Time, with the greatest Address; being the true Cause of their continual Encroachments, and holding their Countries by *Forts,* without settling them. When they come near enough to have Communication with our *Germans,* it will be much more their Interest to plant their Colonies, by offering the said *Germans* easy Settlements, than by bringing new Hands from *Europe*; for by such Means they not only get an Accession of People who are accustomed to the Country, but also weaken us, in Proportion as they strengthen themselves.

That now is the Time they propose to put their grand Scheme in Execution is too evident. They are already so near us, that the *French* Camp, and their Forts upon the *Ohio* and the Parts adjacent, are not more than 225 Miles, horizontal Distance, from the City of *Philadelphia,* and only about two Days March from some of our back Settlements. By Accounts received last Week, they have 2000 effective Men in these Parts, together with a great Body of *Indians* at their Beck.

Having completed his description of the purported French master plan, Smith begins to describe his proposed solution to the crisis. The first element involves the Anglicization of the German immigrants.

Now there is no Way of preventing these dreadful Misfortunes with which we are threatened, but to open the eyes of the *Germans* to their true Interests, and soften this stubborn Genius of theirs, by means of *Instruction*. Faithful Protestant Ministers, and School-masters, should be sent and supported among them to warn them against the Horrors of *Popish* Slavery; to teach them sound Principles of Government, and instruct their Children in the *English* Tongue, and the Value of those Privileges to which they are born among us. If this can be done, and the *French* driven from the *Ohio,* so as to have no Communication with our *Germans* for twenty or thirty Years, till they are taught the Value of the Protestant Religion, understand our Language, and see that they have but one Interest with us; they will for the future bravely fight for their own Property, and prove an impregnable Barrier against the Enemy.

But as if it had been decreed by Fate or the evil Genius of the *Quakers,* that they should never have the same Interest with their Country in a single Instance, it is a Part of their Policy also to oppose every Scheme for instructing and making *Englishmen* of the *Germans.* In order to keep their Seats in the Assembly, they have not only, as I have shown, suffered the *French* to fix themselves on the *Ohio*; they have not only corrupted the Principles of the *Germans*; but, to be consistent with their Interest, they must strive to keep these poor People in the same dark State, into which they have endeavored to sink them. For they know, that if the *Germans* are instructed, so as to be capable of using their own Judgment in Matters of Government, they would no more be misled by the Arts of a *Quaker* Preacher, than of a lurking *French* Priest.

Hence it is that, by means of their hireling Printer, they represent all regular Clergymen as Spies and Tools of the State, telling the People they must not regard any Thing their Ministers advise concerning Elections, since they have a Scheme to elect Men who will bring in a Bill for giving the Tenths to the Clergy, as in some other Countries. It is needless to observe that no such Law can ever be made here, as being repugnant to *Charter*; for our *Quakers,* though they never swear, stick not gravely to affirm and adhere to any Falsehood whatever, provided it will support them in their darling Schemes for Power.

There is nothing they fear more than to see the *Germans* pay any Regard to regular Ministers. Whenever they know of any such Minister in good Terms with his People, they immediately attack his Character by means of this Printer, and distress him by dividing his Congregation, and encouraging Vagabonds and pretended Preachers, whom they every now and then raise up. This serves a double end.

First, According to the Maxim, *divide & impera*—it prevents the People from joining in any new Design, and hinders any Minister from ever having Influence enough to set them right at the annual Elections.

Secondly, By discouraging regular Ministers, it gives the *Quakers* an Opportunity of making more Proselytes.

The Menonists, or Mennonites, are a pacifist sect.

This is the true Reason why the most considerable and wealthy Sect among the *Germans,* is the *Menonists,* whose Principles are much the same with those of the *Quakers;* for they hold it unlawful to take Oaths, or bear Arms. Thus encouraged, by our ruling Men, this Sect has a great influence among the *Germans,* and the *Menonists* are daily increasingly by the Converts they make by their great Wealth, which gives them an Opportunity of paying the Passages of their poor Countrymen, who indent themselves to serve four Years for the Money thus advanced for them.

Besides these, there are near one Fourth of the *Germans* supposed to be Roman Catholics, who cannot be supposed Friends to any Design for defending the Country against the *French.* Many are also *Moravians,* who, as they conceal their Principles, are suspected to be a dangerous People, more especially as they hold some Tenets and Customs, as far as we have any Opportunity of judging of them, very much a-kin to those of the Roman Catholics. There are also many other Sects springing up among the *Germans*; which it would be tedious to name, but most of them are principles against bearing Arms.

Most of the ideas in this paragraph are wild exaggerations; some are totally inaccurate.

I have said enough to show that never was any Country in a more distressed Condition than this; and tho' it has flourished in an extraordinary Degree, as it could not fail to do, when it was young, and all these several Sects employed only in establishing themselves; yet now, when they are grown to Wealth and Maturity, and are not so necessarily employed in their private Concerns, they will turn their Thoughts to the Public, or perhaps against one another; and thence the utmost Confusion must ensue, if a timely Remedy is not applied, and more Checks contrived to balance their increasing Strength then were necessary at first.

I am sorry it has fallen to my Lot to trace all our growing Miseries to the mischievous Policy of my Fellow Subjects, the *Quakers,* who regard no Consequences but holding their own Ground. Truth and Duty obliged me to take up my Pen. We have been too long silent, and had this Representation been made, as it ought to have been, many Years ago, we had not now been in such calamitous Circumstances.

I must, however, in Justice observe that there have been some honest Spirits always among us, who have left nothing unattempted for the Redemption of their Country. Even as late as last *October,* though they knew it was striving against the Stream, those Persons made a noble Effort to convince the *Germans* of our common Danger, and induce them to join in the Choice of Men who would defend the Province, and pay some Deference to his Majesty's Instructions. They reminded the *Germans,* that at their Naturalization, they had solemnly engaged to defend his Majesty's Person and Government against all his Enemies; and that, in case of Refusal, they would be guilty of Perjury. But all was in vain. The *Quakers* held them immoveable, by their usual Insinuations; and we might as soon have attempted to preach the stormy Element into a Calm, as, by Reasoning, to rescue these poor deluded *Germans,* out of the Hands into which they are fallen.

Nevertheless these worthy Persons imagined it their Duty to exert themselves, not only to convince the *Quakers* that their Measures were disapproved of by the better Part of their Fellow-Citizens, but also to satisfy the Government of *England* that there are still many in this Place, who have not banished all Impressions of Loyalty and Duty from their Breasts.

Smith concludes with a plea for intervention.

I can, however, now see no Remedy left among ourselves. We must look to our Mother-Country for Succour, and if it is not speedily granted, this noble Province seems irrecoverably lost. We shall be driven from these beloved Habitations, or else forced to submit once more, not only to civil Slavery, but to Persecution, and that religious Slavery, from which many of our Ancestors left the Land of their Nativity, and sat down in these distant uncultivated Places, amidst the Horrors of the howling Wilderness!

It may be said, with the greatest Justice, that our Proprietors and our late Governors, have done every thing in their Power to assist us, and keep up to an *English* Constitution; for which they have been reviled, abused, and all imaginable Steps taken to hurt them in their Interest, by this perverse and proudest of People, who, under the Mask of extraordinary Sanctity and Conscience, lord it over their Fellow-Subjects.

Whatever be the Consequence, all our Misfortunes can be charges no where but upon our People themselves, and I have shown that it would be plainly repugnant to their Interest to remedy Grievances. All Redress therefore, must, if it comes, come from his Majesty, and the *British* Parliament, to whom our distressed and melancholy Condition must be humbly submitted. If our Case is longer overlooked, I shall soon begin to think of returning, to spend the small Remainder of my Days in *quiet* with you, and to leave my Bones in the Land where I drew my first Breath. Mean while, permit me to assure you, that,

I am, &c.

FINIS.

Deliberations of the Governor's Council, 1756

Scarouyady, an emissary from the Iroquois League, visited Philadelphia in April 1756. He was a familiar figure, having represented the Iroquois at the Philadelphia Treaty of 1742 and the Treaty of Lancaster in 1744. He sought to clarify the Iroquois position in the developing conflict. He also provided advice and information to the governor's council, beginning with a description of Delaware grievances.

SOURCE: "Deliberations of the Governor's Council," in *Minutes of the Provincial Council of Pennsylvania*, vol. 7 (Harrisburg: T. Fenn, 1851), pp. 70–72, 74–76, 79–80.

APRIL 3, 1756

Scarouyady (an Iroquois) speaks

Brother:

You desired us in your Instructions to enquire the particular Reasons assigned by the Delawares and Shawonese for their acting in the manner they do against this Province. I have done it, and all I could get from the Indians is that they heard them say their Brethren the English had accused them very falsly of joining with the French after Colonel Washington's Defeat, and if they would charge them when they were innocent they could do no more if they were guilty; this turned them against their Brethren, and now indeed the English have good Reason for any Charge they may make against them, for they are very heartily their Enemies.

Brethren:

I promised to tell you what passed at the Onondago Council between the Six Nations and the Delaware Deputies, and according to the Information given me by one of the Members present it is as follows, vis': The Council very sharply reprehended the Delawares for their cruel and unbrotherly Behaviour against the English, and earnestly urged them to repent and desist, and the Two Delawares in their Justification spoke thus to the Council:

Uncles:

Your Complaints of us are very true and just, but we hope you will likewise hear what Reasons we have for our Behaviour against the English. When we lived among them they behaved very ill to us; they used us like Dogs; they often saw us pinched with want and starving, and would take not Pity of us; sometimes we were in Liquor, a Fault which you are sensible we cannot always avoid, as we cannot govern ourselves when we come where Liquors are; when we were in this Condition they turned us out of their Houses and beat us, so that when we came to be sober we were not able to get up, and at this very Time they have taken up and put into Prison the few Straglers of our People that are yet among them. Now, Uncles, can this be called Brotherly Treatment? don't you imagine such Usage must raise Ill Nature in our Hearts? And have we not good Reason for what we are doing? We don't doubt if we would let things go on as they have done but would subdue us and make Slaves of us. Nevertheless, Uncles, we listen to what you told us; we thank you for your Advice, and since you insist upon our leaving off we will take what you have said to us and carry it to our Nations and stop them from proceeding. We will tell the Warriors and every one else it is your Pleasure we should not go to War against the English; not a Man shall pass thro' our Town but we will call him to us and make known to him your Command delivered in Council.

The Six Nations, in their Reply, expressed great Resentment at the Delawares; they threatened to shake them by the Head, saying, they were drunk and out of their Senses, and did not consider the consequence of their ill Behaviour, and assured them, that if they did not perform what they promised, they should be severely chastized; whereupon the Delawares again promised to acquaint their Nations with everything that passed, and to send their Answer by Express.

Brother:

This, I hope, will be a sufficient Answer to that Part of your Instructions in which you desire us to enquire and find out the true Reasons of the Delawares turning against us; as to the main Business we had in Charge to lay before the Six Nations, I need not be particular, as I have delivered the several Strings and Belts given us, and every thing done there is put in the Treaty which Col. Johnson sent you by Mr. Claus; by this you will see, that Deputies of the united Nations are gone into the Delaware Country, in order to have a meeting with the Delawares there; and after every thing proposed is agreed upon by those Deputies and our Nephews, you will have their full Answer.

* * *

APRIL 8, 1756

Lieutenant Governor Morris Responds

Brethren, the Six Nations:

Unimpressed, Pennsylvania's lieutenant governor responds with a declaration of war against hostile Indians, an invitation to the Iroquois to join in the effort, and a detailed schedule of scalp bounties. In addition, he announces the intention to build a fort at Shamokin. This would become Fort Augusta, the finest of Pennsylvania's border fortifications.

Your Nephews the Delawares, and some in Alliance with them, have continued, and still do continue, committing the most barbarous and cruel Murders on every part of our Borders, tho' they must certainly have received the Messages from the Onondago Council, by the Two Delawares from Diahoga, ordering them to desist on pain of their displeasure and correction; and it is probable that the second Message of the same Import, from the Great Council held at Fort Johnson, must have been delivered likewise, as Scarroyady says in his Report that the Messengers were set out before he came from thence.

Brethren:

It appears to us that the Delawares have sold themselves to the French, and are determined to take this Opportunity to throw off their Subjection and Dependency upon the six Nations, imagining they shall be supported in it by their New Masters, else they would not have had the Assurance to treat the Six Nations with insolence, as it is well known they have done, even to threaten some of them to their Faces, to make Women of them, if they would not assist them in the War against the English.

Brethren:

We have, by your Advice, taken all the amicable Methods in our power to bring them to desist; you must have been able yourselves to assure the Six Nations, that the Accusations of us were all Groundless, and invented to amuse; and from what you have said in conversation, we think the united Nations saw these false Charges in their true Light, rather as Aggravation than Extenuations of their cousins' Guilt; and we were in hopes their Interposition would have had its weight with the Delawares, and that they would not have dared to continue their Ravages, after receiving their Orders to desist; but you see it is otherwise.

Brethren:

We have remained on the Defensive, waiting for the Result of the Council and your Return; but since neither the Messages we have sent to them, nor these of the Six Nations are of any Avail, and that we have done everything in our power to avoid a War, I now find I can not longer answer it to his Majesty, nor to his Subjects committed to my care, nor to those of the other colonies, to delay any longer to declare them Enemies to his Majesty, and to act against them with all the Vigour possible; I therefore, by this Belt, declare War against the Delawares, and all such as act in conjunction with them. I offer you the Hatchet, and expect your hearty Concurrence with us in this just and necessary War. I not only invite you, but desire you will send this Belt to all your Friends every where, as well on the Sasquehannah, as to the Six Nations and to their Allies, and engage them to join us heartily against these false and perfidious Enemies. I promise you and them Protection and our Assistance, when you shall stand in need of it against your Enemies.

Gave a War Belt.

Brethren:

For the Encouragement of you, and all who will join you in the Destruction of our Enemies, I propose to give the following Bounties or Rewards, Vist.: for every Male Indian Prisoner above Twelve Years Old that shall be delivered to any of the government's Forts, or Towns, One Hundred and Fifty Dollars.

For every Female Indian Prisoner, or male Prisoner of Twelve Years old, and under, delivered as above, one hundred and thirty Dollars.

For the Scalp of every male Indian of above Twelve Years old, one hundred and thirty Dollars.

For the Scalp of every Indian woman, Fifty dollars.

To our own People, I shall observe our own Forms; to you I give the hatchet according to yours. This Belt confirms my Words.

Here gave a Belt.

Brethren:

Agreeable to your repeated Request, I am now going to build a Fort at Shamokin. Forces are raising for that Purpose, and every thing will soon be in readiness. I purpose it as a Place of protection and Refuge for you and your Families, and to this all the Indians who are the Friends of the English may repair, and they will ever find a kind Reception and Necessaries of all kinds.

I need not remind you of your earnest Importunities to have this done, and of your Promise to assist in it. Our Warriors will be animated when they see you join and assist them.

APRIL 10, 1756

Scarouyady responds

Brethren:

It is but the other Day that we had the Happiness to see one another after a long and dangerous Journey, which I am sorry has had no better Effect, and that I could not bring you so good news as you expected. Our Nephews did not listen to us; they were not obedient to what was said to them. We are amazed to find you still sitting with your Hands between your Knees, and for an Apology for so unbecoming a Posture, you tell us, that, as the Delawares were cousins of the Six Nations, you would first consult them, and chose not to act offensively till you should know their minds, as the Delawares are subject to them; you add, now that all means have been tried, and our Cousins are still disobedient, you at last find yourselves under a Necessity to declare War against them.

Brethren:

You have indeed tried all amicable Means with those and with the Six Nations, but as all have proved ineffectual, you do right to strike them. You have had a great deal of Patience; other People on losing a single man, would have armed and drove off the Foe; but you have sat still while numbers of your People have been and now are Murdered. We heartily approve of your Resolutions; awake, shake off your Lethargy; Stand up with your Hatchet in your Hand, and use it manfully. Your Enemies have got great advantage by your Inactivity; Show them you are men.

Brethren:

You told us that you must now build a Fort at Shamokin; we are glad to hear it; it is a good Thing; These young Men are glad in their Hearts, and promise you their Assistance; and would have you go on with it as fast as you can, and others, too, will assist you, when they see you are in earnest. I have good Ground to go upon in what I say; I know what is in the Breasts and Minds of the Warriors of the Mohocks, Oneidas and Oneoquages; they have opened their hearts to me; they are under my command; they will do what I advise, and they shall see this your Belt of Wampum.

Brethren:

The Fort at Shamokin is not a thing of little Consequence; it is of the greatest Importance to us as well as you. Your People are foolish; for want of this Fort, the Indians, who are your friends, can be of no Service to you, having no Place to go to where they can promise themselves Protection. They cannot be called together; they can do nothing for you; they are not secure any where. At present your People cannot distinguish Foes from Friends; they think every Indian is against them; they blame us all without Distinction, because they see nobody appear for them; the common People to a Man entertain this notion, and insult us wherever we go. We bear their ill Usage, tho' very irksome; but all this will be set right when you have built the Fort, and you will see that we in particular are sincere, and many others will come to your assistance. We desire when the fort is built, you will put into the Command of so important a Place some of your People; grave, solid, and sensible Men, who are in Repute amongst you, and in whom we can place a Confidence. Do this, and you will soon see a Change in your Affairs for the better.

Brethren:

As we agree to take up the Hatchet and to come into all your Measures, we must advise you that in all your Steps you will act so as to be secure, and not go forwards for a while and then be obliged to go as far or farther back again, and that with Shame. Your People are foolish; they are extremely heavy, move slow, and are liable to surprize, if you go by yourselves. We are a light Body; we can trip nimbly thro' the Woods, look over a large Extent of Country and see that all is clear, and no Enemy lying concealed to cut you off when you think nothing of it. We must likewise tell you not to make a trifling Peace. You have no doubt heard we are a People who never lay down our Arms; it is true our young People now tell you that they will fight whilst they can find one of the Enemy to fight with, so do not make a trifling Peace. Do yourselves and us Justice, and bring your Enemies to a due Sense of themselves, and to offer just Terms, and then, and not till then, think of a Peace. This is our Advice.

Here they danced the War Dance; the Indian called the Belt singing with a Belt in his hand.

John Armstrong's Account of the Kittanning Fight, 1756

Colonel John Armstrong's official report to the provincial council, which he presented in September 1756, is an exciting, detailed, and well-paced narrative of the fight. He does not pull any punches. For Armstrong, war is a grim business, and he forthrightly addresses desertion, cowardice, and indiscriminate killing.

Some spelling and formatting changes were made for clarity.

SOURCE: "John Armstrong's Account of the Kittanning Fight, 1756," in *Minutes of the Provincial Council of Pennsylvania*, vol. 7 (Harrisburg: T. Fenn, 1851), pp. 257–63.

May it please your Honour:

Agreeable to min of the 29th Ult°, We marched from Fort Shirly the day following, and on Wednesday, the Third Instant, joined our advanced party at the Beaver Dams, a few Miles from Franks Town, on the North branch of Juniata. We were there informed that some of our Men having been out upon a Scout, had discovered the Tracts of two Indians about three Miles on this side of the Alleghenny Mountains, and but a few Miles from the Camp. From the freshness of their Tracts, their killing of a Cub Bear, and the marks of their Fires, it seemed evident they were not twenty-four Hours before us, which might be looked upon as a particular Providence in our Favour that we were not discovered.

Next Morning we decamped, and in two Days came within fifty Miles of the Kittanning. It was then adjudged necessary to send some Persons to reconnoiter the Town and get the best Intelligence they cou'd concerning the Situation and Position of the Enemy; Whereupon an Officer with one of the Pilots and two Soldiers were sent off for that purpose. The day following We met them on their Return, and they informed us that the Roads were entirely clear of the Enemy, and that they had the Greatest Reason to believe they were not discovered; but from the rest of the Intelligence they gave, it appear'd they had not been nigh enough the Town either to perceive the true Situation of it, the Number of the Enemy, or what way it might most advantageously be attacked.

We continued our March, intending to get as near the Town as possible that Night so as to be able to Attack it next Morning about Day Light; but to our great dissatisfaction about nine or ten O'Clock at Night one of our Guides came and told us that he perceived a Fire by the Road side at which he saw two or three Indians a few perches distant from our Front; Whereupon, with all possible Silence, I ordered the rear to retreat about One Hundred perches in order to make way for the Front, that we might consult how we cou'd best proceed without being discovered by the Enemy.

Soon after the Pilot returned a Second Time and assured us from the best observations he cou'd make there were not above Three or Four Indians at the Fire. On which it was proposed that we shou'd immediately surround and cut them off; but this was thought too hazerdous; for if but one of the Enemy had escaped It would have been the Means of discovering the whole design; and the light of the Moon, on which depended our advantageously posting our Men and Attacking the Town, wou'd not admit of our staying until the Indians fell a Sleep. On which it was agreed to leave Lieutenant Hogg with twelve Men and the Person who first discovered the Fire, with orders to watch the Enemy but not to attack them till break of Day, and then if possible to cutt them off. It was also agreed (we believing ourselves to be but about Six Miles from the Town) to leave the Horses, many of them being tired, with what Blankets and other Baggage we then had, and take a Circuit off of the Road, which was very rough and incommodious on Account of the Stones and fallen Timber, in order to prevent our being heard by the Enemy at the Fire place.

This interruption much retarded our March; but a still greater Loss arose from the Ignorance of our Pilots, who neither knew the true Situation of the Town nor the best Paths that lead thereto, By which means, after crossing a Number of Hills and Vallys, our Front reached the River Ohio about one hundred Perches below the main Body of the Town, a little before the Setting of the Moon; To which place, rather than by the Pilots, we were guided by the Beating of a Drum and the Whooping of the Warriors at their Dance. It then become us to make the best use of the remaining Moon light, but are we were aware, an Indian whistled in a very singular manner, about thirty perches from our Front in the foot of a Corn field; upon which we immediately sat down, and after passing Silence to the rear, I asked on Baker, a Soldier, who was our best Assistant, whether that was not a Signal to the Warriors of our Approach? He answered no, and said it was the manner of a Young Fellow's calling a Squa after he had done his Dance, who accordingly kindled a Fire, clean'ed his Gun and shot it off before he went to Sleep. All this time we were Obliged to lay quiet and hush, till the Moon was fairly set. Immediately after, a Number of Fires appeared in different places in the Corn Field, by which Baker said the Indians lay, the Night being warm and that these Fires wou'd immediately be out, as they were only designed to disperse the Gnats.

By this time it was break of day, and the Men having Marched Thirty Miles were most a sleep; the line being long, the three Companies of the Rear were not yet brought over the last precipice. For these some proper Hands were immediately dispatched, and the weary Soldiers being roused to their Feet, a proper Number under sundry Officers were ordered to take the End of the Hill, at which we then lay, and March along the Top of the said Hill, at least one hundred perches, and so much further, it then being day Light, as wou'd carry them Opposite the upper part or at least the Body of the Town. For the lower part thereof and the Corn Field, presuming the Warriors were there, I kept rather the larger Number of the Men, promising to postpone the Attack in that part for Eighteen or Twenty Minutes, until the Detachment along the Hill should have time to Advance to the place Assigned them in doing of which, they were a little unfortunate. The time being elapsed, the Attack was begun in the Corn Field, and the Men with all Expedition possible, dispatched thro' the several parts thereof; a party being also dispatched to the Houses, which were then discovered by the light of the Day.

Captain Jacobs was a prominent Delaware chief who took up the hatchet against the English.

Captain Jacobs immediately gave the War-Whoop, and with Sundry other Indians, as the English Prisoners afterwards told, cried the White Men were at last come, they wou'd then have Scalps enough, but at the same time ordered their Squas and Children to flee to the Woods. Our Men with great Eagerness passed thro' and Fired the Corn Field, where they had several Returns from the Enemy, as they also had from the Opposite side of the River. Presently after, a brisk fire begun among the Houses, which from the House of Captain Jacobs was return'd with a great deal of Resolution; to which place I immediately repaired, and found that from the Advantage of the House and the Port Holes, sundry of our People were wounded, and some killed, and finding that returning the fire upon the House was ineffectual, Ordered the contiguous Houses to be set on Fire; which was performed by Sundry of the Officers and Soldiers, with a great deal of Activity, the Indians always firing, whenever an Object presented it self, and seldom mist of Wounding or killing some of our People; From which House, in moving about to give the necessary Orders and directions, I received a wound from a large Musket Ball in the Shoulder.

Sundry Persons during the Action were ordered to tell the Indians to Surrender themselves prisoners; but one of the Indians, in particular, answered and said, he as a Man and wou'd not be a Prisoner, Upon which he was told in Indian he wou'd be burnt. To this, He answered, he did not care for, he wou'd kill four or five before he died, and had we not desisted from exposing ourselves, they wou'd have killed a great many more, they having a Number of loaded Guns by them. As the fire began to Approach and the Smoak grow thick, one of the Indian Fellows, to shew his Manhood, began to Sing. A Squa, in the same House, and at the same time, was heard to cry and make Noise, but for so doing was severly rebuked by the Men; but by and by the fire being too hot for them, two Indian Fellows and a Squa sprung out and made for the Corn Field, who were immediately shot down by Our People, then surrounding the Houses it was thought Captain Jacobs tumbled himself out at a Garret or Cock loft Window, at which he as Shot; Our Prisoners offering to be Qualified to the Powder horn and Pauch, there taken off him, which they say he had lately got from a French Officer in Exchange for Lieutenant Armstrong's Boots, which he carried from Fort Granvelle, where the Lieutenant [John Armstrong's brother] was killed. The same Prisoners say they are perfectly Assured of his Scalp, as no other Indians there wore their Hair in the same manner. They also say they knew his Squa's Scalp by a particular bob; and also knew the Scalp of a Young Indian called the King's Son.

Before this time Captain Hugh Mercer, who early in the Action was wounded in the Arm, had been taken to the Top of a Hill, above the Town, To whom a number of Men and some of the Officers were gathered, From whence they had discovered some Indians cross the River and take the Hill with an Intent as they thought, to surround us and cut off our Retreat, from whom I had sundry pressing Messages to leave the Houses and retreat to the Hill, or we shou'd all be cut off; but to this cou'd by no means consent until all the Houses were set on fire. Tho' our spreading upon the Hills appeared very necessary, yet did it prevent our Researches of the Corn Field and River side, by which Means sundry Scalps were left behind, and doubtless some Squas, Children, and English Prisoners, that otherwise might have been got.

During the burning of the Houses, which were near thirty in Number, we were agreably entertained with a Quick Sucession of charged Guns, gradually Firing off as reached by the Fire, but much more so, with the vast Explosion of sundry Bags & large Cags of Gunpowder, wherewith almost every House abounded; the Prisoners afterward informing that the Indians had frequently said they had a sufficient stock of ammunition for ten Years War with the English. With the Prooff of Captain Jacob's House, when the Powder blew up was thrown the Leg and Thigh of an Indian with a Child of three or four Years Old, such a height that they appeared as nothing and fell in the adjacent Corn Field. There was also a great Quantity of goods burnt which the Indians had received in a present but ten days before from the French.

By this time I had proceeded to the Hill to have my wound tyed up and the Blood stopped, where the Prisoners which in the Morning had some to our People, informed me that that very day two Battoas of French Men, with a large party of Delaware and French Indians, were to Join Captain Jacobs at the Kittaning, and to set out early the next Morning to take Fort Shirley, or as they called it, George Croghan's Fort, and that Twenty-four Warriors who had lately come to the Town, were set out before them the Evening before, for what purpose thy did not know, whether to prepare Meat, to Spy the Fort, or to make an attack on some of our back Inhabitants.

Soon after, upon a little Reflection, we were convinced these Warriors were all at the Fire we had discovered the Night before, and began to doubt the Fate of Lieutent Hogg and his Party, from this Intelligence of the Prisoners. Our Provisions being Scaffolded some thirty Miles back, except what were in the Men's Haversacks, which were left with the Horses and Blankets with Lieutenant Hogg and His party, and a Number of wounded People then on hand; by the Advice of the Officers it was thought imprudent then to wait for the cutting down of the Corn Field (which was before designed), but immediately to collect our Wounded and force our March back in the best manner we cou'd, which we did by collecting a few Indian Horses to carry off our wounded.

From the Apprehensions of being way laid and surrounded (especially by some of the Woodsmen), it was difficult to keep the Men together, our March for Sundry Miles not exceeding two Miles an Hour, which apprehensions were heightened by the Attempts of a few Indians who for some time after the March fir'd upon each wing and immediately Run off, from whom we received no other Damage but one of our Men's being wounded thro' both Legs. Captain Mercer being wounded, was induced, as we have reason to believe, by some of this Men, to leave the main Body with his Ensign, John Scott, and ten or twelve Men, hey being heard to tell him that we were in great Danger, and that they cou'd take him into the Road a nigh Way, is probable lost, there being yet no Account of him; the most of the Men come in Detachment was sent back to bring him in, but cou'd not find him, and upon the Return of the detachment it was generally reported he was seen with the above Number of Men, take a different Road.

Upon our Return to the place where the Indian Fire had been discovered the Night before, We met with a Sergeant of Captain Mercer's Company and two or three other of his Men who had deserted us that Morning, immediately after the action at Kittaning; These Men on running away had met with Lieut. Hogg, who lay wounded in two different parts of his Body by the Road side; He there told them of the fatal Mistake of the Pilot, who had assured us there were but three Indians at the most at the Fire place, but when he came to attack them that Morning according to the Orders, he found a Number considerably Superior to his, and believe they killed and Mortally wounded three of them the first Fire, after which a warm Engagement began, and continued for above an Hour, when three of his best men were killed and himself twice wounded; the residue fleeing off he was obliged to Squat in a thicket, where he might have laid securely until the main Body had come up, if this Cowardly Sergeant and other that fleed with him had not taken him away; they had marched but a short Space when four Indians appeared, upon which these deserters began to flee.

The Lieutenant then, notwithstanding his wounds, as a Brave Soldier, urging and Commanding them to stand and fight, which they all refused. The Indians pursued, killing one Man and wounded the Lieutenant a third time through the Belly, of which he dyed in a few Hours; but he, having some time before been put on Horse back, rode some Miles from the place of Action But this last Attack of the Indians upon Lieutenant Hogg and the deserters was by then beforementioned Sergeant represented to us in quite different light, he telling us that there were a far larger Number of the Indians there than appeared to them, and that he and the Men with him had fought five Rounds; that he had there seen the Lieutenant and sundry others killed and Scalped, and had also discovered a Number of Indian throwing themselves before us, and insinuated a great deal of such stuff, as threw us into much Confusion, so that the Officers had a great deal to do to keep the Men together, but cou'd not prevail with them to collect what horses and other Baggage that the Indians had left after their Conquest of Lieutenant Hogg and the Party under his Command in the Morning, except a few of the Horses, which some of the bravest of the Men were prevailed on to collect; so that from the mistake of the Pilot, who spied the Indians at the Fire, and the Cowerdice of the said Sergeant and other Deserters, we have sustained a considerable loss of our Horses an Baggage.

It is impossible to ascertain the exact Number of the Enemy killed in the Action, as some were destroy'd by Fire and others in different parts of the Corn Field, but upon a Moderate Computation its generally believed there cannot be less than thirty or Forty killed and Mortally wounded, as much Blood was found in Sundry parts of the Cornfield, and Indians seen in several places crawl into the Weeds on their Hands and Feet, whom the Soldiers, in pursuit of others, then overlooked, expecting to find and Scalp them afterwards; and also several kill'd and wounded in crossing the River.

On beginning our March back we had about a dozen of Scalps and Eleven English Prisoners, but now find that four or five of the Scalps are missing, part of which were lost on the Road and part in possession of those Men who with Captain Mercer seperated from the main Body, with whom also went four of the Prisoners, the other seven being now at this place, where we arrived on Sunday Night, not being ever seperated or attacked thro' our whole March by the Enemy, tho' we expected it every Day.

Upon the whole, had our Pilots understood the true situation of the Town and the Paths leading to it, so as to have posted us at a convenient place, where the Disposition of the Men and the Duty assign'd t them cou'd have been performed with greater Advantage, we had, by divine Assistance, destroy'd a much greater Number of the Enemy, recovered more Prisoners and sustained less damage than what we at present have; but tho' the advantage gained over these our Common Enemy is far from being satisfactory to us, must we not dispise the smallest degrees of Success that God has pleased to give, especially at a time of such general Calamity, when the attempts of our Enemys have been so prevalent and successfull. I am sure there was the greatest inclination to do more, had it been in our power, as the Officers and most of the Soldiers thro' out the whole Action exerted themselves with as much Activity and Resolution as cou'd possibly be expected.

Our Prisoners inform us the Indians have for sometime past talked of fortifying at the Kittanning and other Towns; That the Number of French at Fort Duquesne was about four hundred; that the principle part of their Provisions came up the River from the Mississippi, and that in the Three other Forts which the French have on the Ohio there are not more Men, take them together, than what there are at fort Duquesne.

I hope, as soon as possible, to receive your Honour's Instructions with regard to the Distribution or Stationing of the sundry Companies in this Battalion, and as a Number of Men are now wanting in each of the Companys, whether or not they shall be immediately recruited, and if the sundry Officers are to recruit, that Money be speedily sent for that purpose.

I beg the favour of your Honour, as soon as possible to furnish Governor Morris with a Copy of this Letter, and the Gentlemen Commissioners for the Province with another, as my present indisposition neither admits me to write or dictate any more at this time. In case a Quantity of Ammunition is not already sent to Carlisle, it shou'd be sent as soon as possible, and also if the Companies are to be recruited and compleated, there must be an immediate Supply of about Three hundred Blankets, as there has been a great many lost in the present expedition. Inclosed is a list of the killed and wounded and missing of the Several Companies. I expect to get to Carlisle in about four Days.

I am Your Honour's Most Obedient and most Humble Servant,

JN° ARMSTRONG.

JOHN COX

Testimony of an Escaped Prisoner, 1756

The following selection is an account, given in August 1756, of a Pennsylvanian taken prisoner in a Delaware raid. John Cox was held at Kittannin (or Kittaning), a settlement in the Ohio Country that was successfully attacked by John Armstrong (see p. 127). Shingas and Captain Jacobs were both Delaware war captains from the Ohio Country. The latter was killed in Armstrong's raid.

SOURCE: John Cox, "Testimony of an Escaped Prisoner, 1756," in *Minutes of the Provincial Council of Pennsylvania*, vol. 7 (Harrisburg: T. Fenn, 1851), pp. 242–43.

* * *

Then the Young Man, one John Cox, a Son of the Widow Cox, who had made his Escape from Kittannin, gave the following Information:

That himself, his Brother Richard, and John Craig, in the begining of February last, were taken by nine Deleware Indians from a Plantation two Miles from McDowell's Mill, and carried to the Kittanning Town on the Ohio; that on his way thither he met Shingas with a Party of thirty Men, and afterwards with Captain Jacobs and fifteen, who were going on a Design to destroy the Settlements of Conegocheage; that when he arrived at Kittannin he saw there about one hundred fighting Men of the Deleware Tribe with their Families, and about fifty English prisoners, consisting of Men, Women, and Children; that during his stay there Shingas' and Jacobs' Parties returned—the one with nine Scalps and ten Prisoners, the other with several Scalps and five prisoners, and that another Company of eighteen came from Diahogo with seventeen Scalps fixed on a Pole, and carried them to Fort Du Quesne to obtain their reward; That the Warriors held a council, which with their Warr Dances continued a Week, after which Captain Jacobs went of with a party of Forty-eight Men, intending (as he was told) to fall upon the Inhabitants of Paxton; that the Indians frequently said they resolved to kill all the white Folks except a few, with whom they would afterwards make a Peace; that they made an Example of one Paul Broadly, whom they, agreeable to their usual Cruelty, beat for half an hour with Clubbs and Tomhawks, and afterwards fastning him to a Post crop his head and chopt his Fingers; that they called together all the prisoners to be Witnesses to this Scene of their inhuman Barbarity.

And he further saith that about the Beginning of March he was taken by three Indians to Diahogo, where he found about Fifty Warriors belonging to the Delaware, Mohiccon, & Munsa Tribes, and about Twenty German prisoners; that while he was there the Indians frequently went in parties of twelve to destroy the Inhabitants, and as often returned with their Scalps, but no Prisoners; that their whole conversation was continually filled with Expressions of Vengeance against the English, and resolutions to kill them and lay waste there County; That in May all the Indians removed from Diahogo about Twenty-five Miles higher up the River to plant Corn, where most of them have since lived.

That they, with the prisoners during the whole Summer have been in a starving condition, having very little Venison & Corn, and reduced to the necessity of living upon dog flesh and the few Roots and Berrys they could collect in the Woods; that several of the prisoners have dyed for want of Food; That six Weeks ago about one hundred Indians went off from the Susquehannah to the Ohio for a Supply of Provisions and Amunition, and were expected back in thirty days; That while they were in this distressed Situation they talked several times of making Peace with the English, and many of them observed that it was better to do so than Starve, for that the Rewards the French gave were not sufficient to support them, not having received from them more than one loaf of Bread for each Scalp. But that old Makomesy, his (Cox's) Master, and one of their Chiefs endeavoured to dissuade them from entering into any peaceable Measures with the English, and had constantly encouraged them to continue the War; That while these things were in Agitation in Indian Chief came among them, and informed them that the Mingo's cou'd live with the English and furnished with Provisions and every thing they wanted, while the Delawares were Starving for carrying on the War against them.

The Mingo are ethnically Iroquois people who live in the Ohio Country, but remain outside the authority of the Grand Council in Onondaga. The term Mingo *is derived from an Algonquian word meaning "treacherous" or "stealthy." They generally prefer to be called Ohio Seneca.*

That about thirty days ago he saw several of the Indians going away, with an Intention (as he was informed) to know of the governor of Pennsylvania whether the English wou'd agree to make peace, but that he was told by Makomesy, they were only gone to see whether the English were strong and get Provisions from them.

That on the ninth of August he left Diahogo, and came down the River in a Canoe with Makomsesy to Gnahay, to get some Corn that was left under Ground and that in the Morning, after he arrived there, The Indians having gone out to hunt, he made his Escape on the 14 August last, and came to Fort Augusta at Six O'Clock in the Evening.

The Poor Boy was extreamly reduced, had dangerous Swellings on his body, and was in a Sickly Condition. The Governor, therefore, ordered him lodging and the attendance of a Doctor.

Great Law of the Iroquois League

The Iroquois legend reprinted here features the transformation of the evil and deformed sorcerer Thadodaho (Tha-do-da´-ho´). Two heroes, Hiawatha (Hai-yo^{n}-hwat-hă´) and Deganawidah (De-ka-na-wi-dă), attempt to break his tyranny by clarifying his mind and altering his body with a combination of wampum, songs, and ritual. The eventual success of their efforts reveals the power of these ceremonies.

After curing Thadodaho these rituals unite the original Five Nations into a confederation, which is represented by two metaphors: an extended house and a great tree. The creation of the confederation overcame the legacy of conflict between these peoples by burying the causes of war and creating a commitment to mutual defense. Once the league was founded, council fires were kindled with other nations. According to the Iroquois, neighboring peoples admired the Great Law, but they did not decide to become a part of the confederation.

Many of the ceremonies that transform the bloodthirsty Thadodaho in this legend closely resemble the central rituals of eighteenth-century forest diplomacy. Although peoples other than the Iroquois were not interested in becoming part of the confederation, they did recognize the power and usefulness of the rituals, so they came to dictate treaty protocol. The transformation of Thadodaho demonstrates the confidence that many Indians placed in diplomatic negotiations that followed the proper ritual structure. Rather than an occasion for argument, they hoped that a treaty might facilitate clear thinking, which in turn allowed sympathy and agreement.

The story begins with Thadodaho frustrating the efforts of the people to hold a council in an attempt to throw off his power. He discovers their plans and takes steps to disrupt them. First, he sends a hurricane.

This account was dictated to J. N. B. Hewitt in the late nineteenth century by Ska-na-wa'-tĭ (John Buck), an Onondaga chief living in Ontario. Ska-na-wa'-tĭ recited the legend in Onondaga. This recitation was halting because Ska-na-wa'-tĭ spoke it a few words at a time so that Hewitt could transcribe them accurately. Once he took it down in Onondaga, Hewitt then translated the account into English. Consequently, as Hewitt notes in his introduction, the "legend is rather too concise and sentential than diffuse, and its periods are not so rounded and full as they would be were this legend spoken or related connectedly and without interruption." Still, this version of the Great Law is brief, driving, and straightforward, so it is well suited for use in this game.

SOURCE: J. N. B. Hewitt, "Legend of the Founding of the Iroquois League," *American Anthropologist* 5, no. 2 (April 1892): 131–48.

* * *

In the times of our forefathers it came to pass that although the people unbanked many council-fires they utterly failed to transact any business. Tha-do-da'-ho', the notorious and unscrupulous wizard and tyrant, brought all their plans to nought.

The chiefs of these people sitting in secret session chose, at last, a secluded spot for the purpose of holding a public council, but the wily Tha-do-da'-ho', by means of his spies, who were everywhere, was soon informed of the time and place of the council, and divining that the purpose of the chiefs was to devise means of curbing his despotic power and unbridled passions he resolved to be present at the council.

The place chosen for the council was on the shore of a lake. When the appointed time had come for the council the great wizard and assassinator hastened to be at the chosen place of meeting before all others. Having arrived there, he seated himself facing the lake; there he sat with bowed head, silent but forbidding. He knew that most of the people would come in boats on the lake. Soon many boats, full of people, began to arrive, and the people made their canoes fast and hard by the place where Tha-do-da'-ho' was seated. Whereupon Tha-do-da'-ho', rising to an upright position, stood and in a loud voice called to those people who were still on the lake and said, "Hasten, hurry yourselves, or you will all soon be destroyed. See, a wind is coming, and it may soon cause you all to drown."

The people looked and saw the approaching hurricane, which was unwonted fury. It destroyed all the people who had not landed. The chiefs felt that Tha-do-da′-ho′ had brought on this hurricane by his incantations to do just what it had done, and they one and all said, "Tha-do-da′-ho′ has again defeated all our plans."

Again the chiefs appointed another place and another time for a council. Tha-do-da′-ho′ was, as before, put in possession of the details of the proposed council; this, it was thought, he learned by means of his skill in the occult craft of wizards—of men dealing in the supernatural and superhuman,—but in fact he secured it by means of a band of unscrupulous spies and assassins, who were bound by common interests to do his least bidding.

When the appointed time had arrived for the meeting a vast concourse of people assembled at the chosen place. The people constructed temporary cabins or lodges near that of the great chief Hai-yo^n-hwat-hă′. Then it was found that their great adversary was present also, which had a depressing effect upon all the people, for they all feared the blood-thirsty Tha-do-da′-ho′, whose vengeance when provoked knew no bounds and respected no ties of blood.

The daughter of Hai-yo^n-hwat-hă′ went a short distance in the forest to gather fagots for her fire, when Tha-do-da′-ho′ seeing her looked skywards and shouted, "Look ye up; some living thing is falling. What is it?" All eyes were now upturned, and they saw a beautiful creature flying down toward the place where the daughter of Hai-yo^n-hwat-hă′ was gathering wood. She at once took up her bundle of fagots and started for her lodge, but now all the people were rushing forward to see the falling object, and in the tumult the daughter of Hai-yo^n-hwat-hă′, being great with child, was knocked down and trampled on by the onrushing mass of people.

It was afterwards found that she had been trodden to death, to the great sorrow of her father, Hai-yo^n-hwat-hă′. In his great grief he exclaimed, "It has gone ill with us; all my children are now gone from me; they have been destroyed by Tha-do-da′-ho′, and he has spoiled all our plans. It now behooves me to go abroad among other people. I will start now. 'I will *split-the-sky*.' "

Then he entered the forest, and going directly south crossed the Onondaga Mountain. As he traveled he came to a lake, and followed its shore until he came to the middle of it—that is, to a point midway from the ends of the lake—and there he stood and looked and saw a multitude of ducks floating on the surface of the lake. Addressing himself to the ducks, Hai-yo^n-hwat-hă′ called out in a loud voice, saying, "Attend ye to this matter, ye floating boats." Thereupon the multitude of ducks flew up, taking up with them all the water in the lake. Hai-yo^n-hwat-hă′ went a short distance into the now empty lake and began to dig into the mud, and took therefrom a small quantity of wampum which he placed in his traveling pouch.

Then arising he again took up his journey, and having gone a short distance and after crossing a mountain he stopped and said, "This place shall be called Onondeyă′$_x$ne." Then, changing his course, he turned and went eastward. He pursued this direction until he came to a place covered with a young growth of tall hickory trees. Here he halted and said, "This place shall be called Onĕñnukaes′ke."

Having passed this place, he finally came to a cabin and entered it. The man of the cabin said to him, "My unfortunate younger brother, Hai-yo^n-hwat-hă′, what evil thing has come to pass that causes you to wander purposelessly in thy greatness?"

Hai-yo^n-hwat-hă′, answering, said, "Tha-do-da′-ho′ is mad. He has destroyed my three children. They were all I had, and Tha-do-da′-ho′ has slaughtered them."

Then the owner of the cabin said, "You must remain here now. We will possess this place equally. You shall learn what matters are being discussed by the chiefs."

So for some time he abode there with his host; but nothing was ever told him of what the chiefs were discussing in their councils, and the mind of Hai-yo^n-hwat-hă′ was greatly troubled. Finally he left the cabin in silence and went into a field of growing corn, where he found a temporary lodge of bark. In it he seated himself and, binding a belt of wampum about his head and taking a bundle of wampum strings, he sang a song, saying, "Some very vainglorious people say, 'thou and I will possess these things equally; you shall know what things are transpiring in council; but only falsely have they spoken.' "

He was aware that some one was listening to what he said. The person who had heard what he sang ran quickly to the cabin and related what he had seen and heard. The chief said, "Go, bring him back into the house." When they reached the temporary lodge Hai-yo^n-hwat-hă′ had gone.

Having resumed his journey, he traveled on until he came to another cabin, which he entered. The host said to him, "Hai-yo^n-hwat-hă′, what has happened that you wander purposelessly in your greatness, for you are worthy of the highest homage?"

Hai-yo^n-hwat-hă′ replied, "Tha-do-da′-ho′ is mad. He is angry and rages. Thence I have come. My three children have perished. Tha-do-da′-ho′ destroyed them, and then I came away. I was angry and troubled. I *split-the-sky* in my journey."

At that the host said, "In what kind of place does Tha-do-da′-ho′ abide?"

Hai-yo^n-hwat-hă′ replied, "From it smoke arises upward until it touches the sky. There Tha-do-da′-ho′ dwells."

The host answered, "I will inform the chiefs concerning this; perhaps they may have something to say upon the matter."

Then De-ka-na-wi-dă, for it was he who lived there, requested Hai-yo^n-hwat-hă′ to remain with him, and he laid the matter, as he had promised, before the council to learn its judgment regarding it.

After discussing the matter for a time the chiefs finally decided to wait upon Tha-do-da′-ho′. Replying, De-ka-na-wi-dă said, "If so, then produce your wampum-strings;" but they had none. To remedy this they began stringing common shells on threads of skin to represent twelve matters or themes.

At this juncture De-ka-na-wi-dă said, "Hai-yo^{n}-hwat-hă′, what theme or matter can you add to what we have?"

Hai-yo^{n}-hwat-hă′, taking up his pouch of wampum-strings, said, "This that I hold in my hand is what I will contribute."

Thanking him, De-ka-na-wi-dă said, "The thing which we shall customarily use hereafter is now complete. This shall endure for all time." Out of the pouch thirteen wampum-strings, representing thirteen matters or themes, were taken out, and they placed them on a horizontal pole or rod.

They gazed upon the array of wampum-strings and were very greatly pleased, exclaiming, "We will use these in our work. They will be of great benefit to us." Then the wampum was placed in parcels. Te-ka-ĭq′-ho’-kĕ^{n} had one, Hai-yo^{n}-hwat-hă′ one, and Tcă′-te-ka-ĭq′-hwa-te′ one, making three persons.

Then they said, "It is now our duty to work. We must go to the place where Tha-do-da′-ho′ abides. We will straighten and reconstruct his mind, so that he may again have the mind of a human being."

"Let us," said De-ka-na-wi-dă, "express our gratitude." In doing this he said, "*Yo-qhĕñ′———*;" to which the assembled chiefs rejoined, "*Hi-yā′———*." Then De-ka-na-wi-dă sang solemnly, saying, "*Hai-i, hai-i, hĭ-i, ka-ya′-ne-ĕ^{n} tes-ke-no^{n}-hĕñ′-ne′: hai-i, hai-i, hĭ′-i, ka-ya′-ne’-ĕ^{n} tes-ke-no^{n}-hĕñ′-ne′*," etc., etc., of what is called the Six Songs. De-ka-na-wi-dă then said, "This shall be observed as a custom for all time. They shall sing the Six Songs as occasion requires, for the prosperity and common weal of all."

De-ka-na-wi-dă continued, "Who will go to seek the smoke of Tha-do-da′-ho′?"

Tai′-he said, "I will go;" but De-ka-na-wi-dă said, "It would not be auspicious for us to have you go. Two persons are required to go."

Then two men said, "We are willing to go."

De-ka-na-wi-dă replied, "You two will be acceptable messengers."

That night the two spies started on their journey, and when they reached the end of the clearing surrounding the council-house they transformed themselves into crows and flew on their journey of discovery, passing over the tops of forests, watching and carefully scanning the horizon to find the smoke they were commissioned to seek. Finally they saw a smoke arising, and they flew toward the place whence it arose, and, assuming again the human shape, they entered the cabin and found that it was not the abode of Tha-do-da′-ho′. The master of the cabin said to them, "I place myself like a great tree-trunk in the path of De-ka-na-wi-dă, so that whatever he may intend to do he will find me in his path, lying there, so that he must take me with him in his enterprise. If you two find the smoke, pass this way on your return trip and let me know what you have learned about the smoke and fire of Tha-do-da′-ho′, the wizard."

When night had come, the two spies, with assurances to their host that they would report to him the success or failure of their errand, left the cabin. As they reached the limits of the forest they again transformed themselves into crows and flew over the forests, intently scanning the horizon in all directions to discover, if possible, the smoke of Tha-do-da´-ho´. After a long search they found a smoke rising like a huge pillar to the very sky. When they reached the borders of the forest surrounding the place where they saw the smoke arising, they assumed again their human form, and entered the long-house whence issued the smoke. Upon entering the door, they immediately asked if that was the abode of Tha-do-da´-ho´, and the astonished by-standers, in a loud warning whisper said, *"Tcĭ, tcĭ, tcĭ, tcĭ,"* to enjoin silence upon them, as it was death to any one who so far forgot himself as to speak louder than a soft whisper in the presence of the sorcerer.

Finally, the two spies discover the lodge of the horrible wizard, who they found wrapped up in his gigantic penis (which this translation delicately refers to as his "membrum virile").

Then the inmates of the long house pointed to the shape which represented the wizard in the flesh. The two spies looked and they were struck speechless and motionless by seeing a thing—a shape—that was not human but rather supernatural and deformed; for the hair of Tha-do-da´-ho´ was composed of writhing, hissing serpents, his hands were like unto the claws of a turtle, and his feet like unto bear's claws in size and were awry like those of a tortoise, and his body was cinctured with many folds of his *membrum virile*—truly a misshapen monster.

The two spies quickly left the place, and when they had reached the forest they resumed their crow-forms, and then flying back to the first-found smoke, they stopped there, as they had promised, and related what they had seen around the council-fire of Tha-do-da´-ho´. The head-chief, who was their former host, again said to them, "I place myself across the path of De-ka-na-wi-dă like a great tree-trunk; so that whatever De-ka-na-wi-dă may decide to do, he must take me up with him."

Having fulfilled their promise, the two messengers resumed their journey homeward, and very soon reached their home, for they flew in the form of crows. Upon their arrival De-ka-na-wi-dă asked, "Did you two find the smoke?"

They answered, "We found the smoke. The thing we saw was horrifying. Tha-do-da´-ho´ is not human; he is daimonic and supernatural."

De-ka-na-wi-dă, replying, said, "We must go to the place where Tha-do-da´-ho´ abides. It is our duty to endeavor to reconstruct his mind, so that he shall again have the mind of a human being. If we can accomplish this great work we shall be fortunate, and we shall reap fruitful benefits from it. In this enterprise we must use the 'thirteen matters' or 'topics.' Now, let us go where Ni-ha-yeñ-ta´-ko´-na (the Great Tree) lives, and when we arrive there we shall say, Now we have come. It is necessary that we two shall work together.' Now then, let us go to the place where Tha-do-da´-ho´ dwells."

All assented, saying, "Let us now take up our journey."

The leader, De-ka-na-wi-dă, then said, "When we have reached or destination, the habitation of Tha-do-da′-ho′, we shall make a fire for him 'at the wood's edge.' We will speak to him and we shall hail him by congratulatory words. We will also tell him that we have a matter in which he is concerned; but this latter shall come to pass in the 'Principal Place.' "

Having completed their labors here, they took up their journey, singing as they went the song called *At-ha-hi-no^n′-ke*. * * *

Finally they arrived at the edge of the forest where the underbrush grew in dense clusters; they were now near their destination. Hai-yo^n-hwat-hă′ said to his companions, "We are now at our journey's end," and immediately they halted.

Whereupon De-ka-na-wi-dă said, "Let us now send some one to notify them of our arrival." This was done.

The messenger notified the resident councilors of their arrival, saying, "They ordered me their cane to come here; they have kindled their fire at the *edge of the woods*, and there we will meet, beside the thorny underbrush."

The resident chiefs went to the place where the fire had been kindled, and there they met the visiting chiefs. Then the preliminary business, called *o-hĕñ′-toñ′ ka-ĭq-hwa-teq′-kwĭ oñ-tat-noñ-hĕñ*, "the preliminary part in which mutual greetings are had." Immediately after kindling a fire at the *edge of the woods*, the new-comers began to sing the Six Songs. Tha-do-da′-ho′ heard the singing and immediately a radical change came over his mind, for he was gladdened—transfigured—by the singing.

When they had sung the Six Songs they said, "And now we will speak what we have to say. We will begin with his mind; we will change it into that of a human being. While we are making our address we will hold in our hand the short string of wampum; we will also give him the Sea Gulls' wing [Ska-yes-ko′nă], which will be one of the first things to be done, for by this the land shall be preserved free from dirt and evil things. *He* will then meditate in peace and contentment. We will wean him from his ungovernable temper of mind, and we will cast it deep in the ground away from him. His hands we will mend and adjust, so that they will be like those of other men; his hair of living serpents we will change from its snakehood, so that his hair may be like that of other men; and his hands, awry and misshapen as they are, we will make like those of a human being; his feet also, deformed and unnatural as they are, we will change to the shape common to those of other men, and, lastly, that with which he is trussed, his *membrum virile*, we will reduce to its proper length and size—we will make it six thumb widths in length."

When these salutations were ended they said, "Let us go to the Principal Place. The war chief will take them by the arm to conduct them thither."

Arriving there, De-ka-na-wi-dă arose and said, "My pitiable brother Hai-yo^n-hwat-hă′ [this was the first time in a long time that they had heard the name] came to my house. Moreover, he brought with him a matter of importance which he related to me. Does Tha-do-da′-ho′ dwell in this place?"

The inmates of the place whispered precatively, *"Tcĭ, tcĭ, tcĭ, tcĭ,"* to silence him, and only one of them dared to point him out with his finger. The visitors looked and were horrified. They saw Tha-do-da′-ho′; he looked to be anything but human, for his hands were like the feet of a turtle, his feet like those of a bear, and his head, in lieu of hair, was wreathed and adorned with writhing and hissing serpents.

Undaunted, De-ka-na-wi-dă said, "We are now here. We came seeking Tha-do-da′-ho′. Now, chiefs, unwrap again your *matters*." Obedient to this command they took the wampum strings out of the pouch one by one, thirteen in number, representing as many matters of importance and moment, and they placed them in order on a horizontal rod. This done, De-ka-na-wi-dă said, "Let us express our thanks, for this is now being completed." He then sang the Six Songs, saying:

"Hai-i, hai-i, hĭ-i, hai-i, hai-i, hĭ-i, hai-i, hai-i, hĭ-i;
"Hai-i, hai-i, hĭ-i, khe-ya′-wě^n tes-khe-no^n-hěñ′-ne′;
    my off-spring I-come-to-greet-them-again;
"Hai-i, hai-i, h'ĭ-i, O-yě^n'-koñ′-do^n tes-khe-no^n-hěñ′-ne′;
    the war-chiefs I-come-to-greet-them-again;
"Hai-i, hai-i, hĭ-i, wa'-koñ′-ne′ kĭ" tes-khe-no^n-hěñ-ne′;
    the-body-of-women I-come-to-greet-*them*-again;
"Hai-i, hai-i, hĭ-i, hak-so′-tă ho-ti-ĭq-hwak′-neq;
    my-grand-parents it-was-their-work;
"Hai-i, hai-i, hĭ-i, hak-so′-tă tci-yat-hon-te′-nyoñk;"
    my-grand-parents do-ye-continue-to-listen-to-them.

When these Six Songs were being sung Tha-do-da′-ho′ listened attentively to them and even manifested a feeling of pleasure. Lastly, he raised his horrid head, an act he had never been known to do. Whereupon De-ka-na-wi-dă, elated by this propitious sign of mental regeneration, exclaimed, "So let it come to pass. What we have undertaken is being accomplished in the manifestation of returning reason and anthropic feelings."

Then Tha-do-da′-ho′ spoke and said, "It gave me great pleasure to hear the singing of the Six Songs."

Again arising, De-ka-na-wi-dă continued, "We have come here seeking a certain person; we seek Tha-do-da′-ho′. The mind that belongs to his body is not now that of a human being." Then, taking his station near Tha-do-da′-ho′, the speaker continued, "Now, we will reconstruct and straighten out thy mind.

Hai-i, hai-i, hĭ-i, hai-i, hai-i, hai-i, hai-i, a-ke-wi′-yo e-koñ-he-wa′-tha′."
my-beautiful-thing, (it-is)-a-besom.

Having repeated this song thrice, the speaker delivered a string of wampum and said, "This song hereafter shall belong to you alone. It is called 'I-use-it-to-beautify-the-earth.' "

It was now evident that the mind of Tha-do-da'-ho' had experienced a change. De-ka-na-wi-dă, however, continued, "There is yet another thing which it is our purpose to make straight and natural, and that is thy body. Thy feet are awry and misshapen. It was intended that the parts of the body of man should be natural in size and shape." Then passing his hand over Tha-do-da'-ho''s feet, they instantly assumed the natural form of human feet, and he delivered another string of wampum.

Continuing, De-ka-na-wi-dă said, "There is yet another thing to be made natural. We will now restore the shape of thy hands, also awry and deformed. Your hands shall [passing his hands over them] now be like those of men," and delivered another string of wampum.

Still speaking, De-ka-na-wi-dă said, "It was not intended that men should have snakes in lieu of hair," and brushing them from his head and casting them away, he added, "Thy head shall now be like that of a human being;" he then delivered another wampum-string.

"One other thing remains," said De-ka-na-wi-dă; "it was not intended that this should be thus," and then unwinding from the body of Tha-do-da'-ho' the many fathoms of the *membrum virile* with which he was girdled many times and measuring with the eye its natural length, De-ka-na-wi-dă cut away the excessive length saying, "This shall be so long," and held in his hand a wampum-string as he spoke and then delivered it, but when he let go the cut member, there was dermal recession. He made three several attempts to reduce the recession, delivering every time a string of wampum, but he failed.

Then the chiefs said, "Although this will not submit, yet it will not now have the potency to kill a person; hence, leave it; it will make no more trouble." Thus they made and changed Tha-do-da'-ho' into a natural man.

When they had accomplished this great work they exclaimed—"We have now redeemed Tha-do-da'-ho'. Everything will now prosper in a natural and peaceful manner. It is now our duty to work, first, to secure to the nations peace and tranquility."

De-ka-na-wi-dă and Hai-yo^{n}-hwat-hă' then added, "We must now work for the good of the Commonwealth and its laws as our second great object. We rejoice that we have been able to do what we have accomplished. We must labor continuously on the law and the Commonwealth. We must now work on that which is the guarantee of our welfare and which is on the greatest moment and importance. Are there not nights when there is danger that one may kill another, to our mischief? It is this matter which we must set right, so that the nations of Natural Man may dwell in peace and tranquility, undisturbed by the shedding of blood.

The term Natural Man *is the literal translation of the contemporary Iroquois word for "Indian": Oñ-kwe-hoñ-we.*

"In the first place, the chiefs must be patient, long-suffering, and courageous in the cause of right and equity. This applies to the chiefs and the war-chiefs who shall fill these offices. All this must be done for the sole object of peace and quietness. We are bound also to carry this Law around and show it to all the nations, and we will name it the Great Law—the Great Law of Equity; for all, all the nations without exception, hate us of the 'Extended-House.' Besides, it is a fact that battle-axes are crossed and men are slaughtering one another; so now we have put this evil from the earth. We have cast it deep down into the earth. Into one bundle have we gathered the causes of war, and have cast this bundle away. Yea, we even uprooted a tall pine tree, making a very deep hole in the earth; and at the bottom of this hole runs a swift water-current. Into this current have we thrown the causes of wars and strife. Our great-grandchildren shall not see them, for we have set back in its former place the great tall pine tree.

"Again, we have shaded ourselves under a gigantic tree with very long leaves. This tree we ourselves have set up. Under it we will habitually rest in the shadow of its great leaves, because the shade of it will be pleasant and beautiful. This thing as well: All the nations will look upon the Law, and all Natural Mankind will like and desire it. Never again shall we be in fear. All the nations of Natural Mankind will then dwell in peace and tranquility, for they all have placed their minds there—have given their allegiance to it. Wampum was given by them to confirm their words and to preserve them as well. They all became of one mind, and they were rejoiced and happy. Now we have formed ourselves—the nations—into one round and compact body. We have also taken one another by the hands and arms. We have put our minds in one place. This has been done. Furthermore, we must have but one head, one tongue, and but one blood in our bodies.

Once the Iroquois Confederation was formed, steps were taken to set up regular diplomatic ties with neighboring peoples. This included the Tceroki (or Cherokee), Huron, Wyandot, and the "Seven Nations living towards the sunrising," which included the Lenâpé (or Delaware). The league is described here in an open-ended way, allowing for future members and promising terrible retribution against those who take up the hatchet against the league. His work done, Deganawidah provides a few final admonitions and dies.

"More than this, we have erected a tree which has put forth a Great White Root which goes toward the west, the sunsetting; another which goes toward the sunrising, the east; another which goes toward the mid-sky, the south; another which goes toward the place of cold, the north. These are the Roots of the Law of Natural Men. Upon these the tree stands and spreads forth its branches. On its top sits a bird, named Ska-ji-e'-nă' (the eagle). It stands alone in its unrivaled eyesight, being in this respect unequaled by any other thing. This bird keeps a lookout in all directions, and should it see approaching us that which will be our death and destruction it will inform us thereof. Some time, perhaps, we may be in a deplorable condition. This will have the power to aid us in our need. A council-fire in behalf of this Law shall be kindled for all nations. Such a fire shall be lighted for the Tcerokis and one as well for the Thăs-tă-he-tcĭ, or the Hurons and Wyandots, so that all may work out this Law and so that the purpose of having all Natural Men receive this Law may be executed. We shall also kindle such a fire for the Seven Nations living toward the sunrising, so that they can work in behalf of this Law, and in their turn light such fires among the nations living still farther toward the east than they do." De-ka-na-wi-dă then ceased speaking.

The Seven nations did light such fires for the nations living still farther toward the sunrising. All received the Great Law, and worked together for the good and welfare of all Natural Men. Then men went toward the south, visiting the Tcerokis in behalf of this Law, and a council-fire of this Law was lighted for them. These men then went toward the west, where they kindled similar fires for the Tyo-non-ta-te′-ka′ (Tionontates) and the Thăs-tă-he-tcĭ (Wyandots). All these nations received this Law—this fire of the council-fire of the Extended-House (of the Iroquois).

Then they said, "We have completed our task. Nevermore will any one hear it said, 'There lie the bodies of persons who have been assassinated;' that is the matter which we have accomplished, which is to work in the Law to secure to all the nations peace and prosperity, to secure to all Men of Nature for all time the benefits of living in peace; that all affairs and matters shall be left to the judgment of the chiefs for their decision; that this may endure for all time, that they shall work according to the Great Law upon which we have built this structure. And when this matter will extend itself in all directions, there may be some who will not be willing to receive it, but we shall not be reprehensible, since we have offered it to them—to the nations of Natural Men living alongside any Great White Root of the Great Law. We have likewise laid our heads upon these Roots for mutual protection. It may be that at some future time we may become few and feeble, then we must go to find a great elm tree for a support. It may be that after the lapse of time some person may come and will see this Root (or, one of these roots) extending along, and seeing that it is a Root beautiful beyond measure, will raise his hatchet and will strike it into the Root—blood will flow from the Root, we all shall feel it. Whenever we have felt this, we shall know that he who has struck his hatchet into the Root does not desire to receive the Great Law. Then we will look and we shall see the back of the retreating culprit, and before he has gone far something occult and supernatural will happen to him, for blood shall come forth from his mouth, and there will be yet power to repeat this mystic stroke upon him. Whosoever will thus use his hatchet does not like the Great Law belonging to the various tribes of Natural Men."

De-ka-na-wi-dă now said, "We have thus completed this whole matter. Permit me to say to you, apply yourselves diligently to all the duties you have taken upon yourselves; faithfully perform every responsibility, because to you is entrusted the preservation and settlement of all things. My mind will now grow in the fruition of pleasure and contentment. Moreover, there shall be signs for identification as to those who shall become chiefs. Thus, besides, we will give the tokens and symbols thereof. So we will add thereto the horns by which they may be known—by which they shall be distinguished from all others—so that they can say, 'These are chiefs.' "

When their labors were at an end, De-ka-na-wi-dă, resuming his address, said, "Let my name never be named (as an official of the League). No one shall be appointed to succeed me, as others can advise you; but having founded the Extended-House, a work which no other person could have done, I shall be seen no more of any man." Then, crossing through the Extended-House, he went to *Sta-te'*; there he lies buried, his grave being lined and his body being covered two spans deep with hemlock boughs.

* * *

In the Iroquois telling, everyone loved the Great Law.

Then, after they had constructed the Extended-House, they carried this Law to all the nations of Natural Man. In prosecuting the work among these peoples we declare that we have absolved ourselves from the things by means of which persons are killed, because we desire that there shall be continual peace, that no one shall see another person murdered. Moreover, all the nations who looked upon this Law as it was borne about by the chiefs were captivated and enamored by it; they all agreed that it was good—that it was promotive of good. They liked it so well that they vowed, saying "I place my mind on the wampum." So they all loved it. Then the chiefs said, "Let us then make one mind in which all nations of Natural Man shall be contained. Let this be in accordance with our form and kind of Law. Now, then, let us join hands so firmly that should a tree fall on them they would not become disjoined. Now, we all have put our minds in one place, and in addition we will now have but one soul, but one head, and but one tongue shall be in us; so that the nations of Natural Man shall be of one mind."

* * *

SELECTED BIBLIOGRAPHY

SECONDARY SOURCES

Anderson, Fred. *Crucible of War: The Seven Years' War and the Fate of Empire in British North America, 1754–1766*. New York: Vintage, 2000.

Aquila, Richard. *The Iroquois Restoration: Iroquois Diplomacy on the Colonial Frontier, 1701–1754*. Lincoln: University of Nebraska Press, 1997.

Auth, Stephen F. *The Ten Years' War: Indian-White Relations in Pennsylvania, 1755–1765*. New York: Garland, 1989.

Axtell, James, ed. *The Indian Peoples of Eastern America: A Documentary History of the Sexes*. New York: Oxford University Press, 1981.

Barbour, Hugh, and J. William Frost. *The Quakers*. New York: Greenwood, 1988.

Barr, Daniel P. *A Colony Sprung from Hell: Pittsburgh and the Struggle for Authority on the Western Pennsylvania Frontier, 1744–1794*. Kent, OH: Kent State Press, 2014.

Barr, Daniel P. "'This Land Is Ours Not Yours': The Western Delawares and the Seven Years' War in the Upper Ohio Valley, 1755–1758." In *The Boundaries between Us: Natives and Newcomers along the Frontiers of the Old Northwest Territory, 1750–1850*, Daniel P. Barr, ed. Kent, Ohio: Kent State, 2006, pp. 25–43.

Becker, Marshall Joseph. "Lenopi; Or, What's in a Name? Interpreting Evidence for Cultures and Cultural Boundaries in the Lower Delaware Valley." *Bulletin of the Archaeological Society of New Jersey* 63 (2008): 11–32.

Brumwell, Stephen. *Redcoats: The British Soldier and War in the Americas, 1755–1763*. New York: Cambridge University Press, 2006.

Calloway, Colin G. *Pen & Ink Witchcraft: Treaties and Treaty Making in American Indian History*. Oxford & New York: Oxford University Press, 2013.

Campbell, Alexander V. *The Royal American Regiment: An Atlantic Microcosm, 1755–1772*. Norman: University of Oklahoma Press, 2010.

Daiutolo, Robert Jr. "The Role of Quakers in Indian Affairs during the French and Indian War." *Quaker History* 77, no. 1 (spring 1988): 1–30.

Dowd, Gregory Evans. *A Spirited Resistance: The North American Indian Struggle for Unity, 1745–1815*. Baltimore, MD, & London: Johns Hopkins University Press, 1992.

Fenton, William N. *The Great Law and the Longhouse: A Political History of the Iroquois Confederacy*. Norman: University of Oklahoma, 1998.

Foster, Michael K. "Another Look at the Function of Wampum in Iroquois-White Councils." In *The History and Culture of Iroquois Diplomacy: An Interdisciplinary Guide to the Treaties of the Six Nations and Their League*, ed. Francis Jennings. Syracuse, NY: Syracuse University Press, 1985.

Foster, Michael K. "On Who Spoke First at Iroquois-White Councils: An Exercise in the Method of Upstreaming." In *Extending the Rafters: Interdisciplinary Approaches to Iroquoian Studies*. Michael K. Foster, Jack Campisis, and Marianne Mithun, eds. Albany: State University of New York Press, 1984.

Fur, Gunlög. *A Nation of Women: Gender and Colonial Encounters among the Delaware Indians*. Philadelphia: University of Pennsylvania Press, 2009.

Grenier, John. *The First Way of War: American War Making on the Frontier*. Cambridge & New York: Cambridge University Press, 2008.

Grimes, Richard S. *The Western Delaware Indian Nation, 1730–1795: Warriors and Diplomats*. Bethlehem, PA: Lehigh University Press, 2017.

Harley, Lewis R. *The Life of Charles Thomson: Secretary of the Continental Congress and Translator of the Bible from the Greek*. Philadelphia: George W. Jacobs, 1900.

Hirst, Margaret E. *Quakers in Peace and War: An Account of their Peace Principles and Practice*. London: Swarthmore Press, 1923.

Hinderaker, Eric. "Declaring Independence: The Ohio Indians and the Seven Years' War." In *Cultures in Conflict: The Seven Years' War in North America,* Warren R. Hofstra, ed. Lanham, MD: Rowman & Littlefield, 2007, pp. 105–25.

Hinderaker, Eric. *Elusive Empires: Constructing Colonialism in the Ohio Valley, 1673–1800*. Cambridge: Cambridge University Press, 1997.

Hinderaker, Eric, and Peter C. Mancall. *At the Edge of Empire: The Backcountry in British North America*. Baltimore, MD: Johns Hopkins University Press, 2003.

Hunter, Charles E. "The Delaware Nativist Revival of the Mid-Eighteenth Century." *Ethnohistory* 18, no. 1 (winter 1971): 39–49.

James, Sydney V. *A People among Peoples: Quaker Benevolence in Eighteenth-Century America*. Cambridge: Harvard University Press, 1963.

Jennings, Francis. *Benjamin Franklin, Politician: The Mask and the Man*. New York & London: Norton, 1996.

Jennings, Francis. "The Delaware Interregnum," *Pennsylvania Magazine of History and Biography* 89: 2 (April 1965): 174–98.

Jennings, Francis. *Empires of Fortune: Crowns, Colonies & Tribes in the Seven Years War in America*. New York & London: Norton, 1988.

Jennings, Francis. "Iroquois Alliances in American History." In *The History and Culture of Iroquois Diplomacy: An Interdisciplinary Guide to the Treaties of the Six Nations and Their League*. Francis Jennings, ed. Syracuse, NY: Syracuse University Press, 1985.

Johansen, Bruce E. " 'By Your Observing the Methods Our Wise Forefathers Have Taken, You Will Acquire Fresh Strength and Power': Closing Speech of Canassatego, July 4, 1744, Lancaster Treaty." In *Native American Speakers of the Eastern Woodlands: Selected Speeches and Critical Analyses*, Barbara Alice Mann, ed. Westport, CT: Praeger, 2001.

Jordan, John W. "William Parsons: Surveyor General and Founder of Easton, Pennsylvania." *Pennsylvania Magazine of History and Biography* 33 (1909): 340–46.

Kalter, Susan, ed. *Benjamin Franklin, Pennsylvania, and the First Nations: The Treaties of 1736–62*. Urbana: University of Illinois Press, 2006.

Kraft, Herbert C. *The Lenape-Delaware Indian Heritage 10,000 BC to AD 2000*. Stanhope, NJ: Lenape Books, 2001.

McConnell, Michael N. "Peoples 'in between': The Iroquois and the Ohio Indians, 1720–1768." In *Beyond the Covenant Chain: The Iroquois and Their Neighbors in Indian North America, 1600–1800,* Daniel K. Richter and James H. Merrell, eds. Syracuse, NY: Syracuse University Press, 1987.

McConnell, Michael N. *A Country Between: The Upper Ohio Valley and Its Peoples, 1724–1774*. Lincoln & London: University of Nebraska Press, 1992.

Merrell, James H. *Into the American Woods: Negotiators on the Pennsylvania Frontier*. New York & London: Norton, 1999.

Merrell, James H., ed. *The Lancaster Treaty of 1744 with Related Documents*. Boston: Bedford/St. Martin's, 2008.

Merritt, Jane T. "Metaphor, Meaning, and Misunderstanding: Language and Power on the Pennsylvania Frontier." In *Contact Points: American Frontiers from the Mohawk Valley to the Mississippi, 1750–1830,* Andrew R. L. Clayton and Fredrika J. Teute, eds. Chapel Hill: University of North Carolina Press, 1998.

O'Toole, Fintan. *White Savage: William Johnson and the Invention of America*. New York: Farrar, Straus & Giroux, 2005.

Otto, Paul. "Wampum," In *Encyclopedia of Native American History,* Peter Mancall, ed. New York: Facts on File, 2011, pp. 921–23.

Otto, Paul. "*Wampum:* The Transfer and Creation of Rituals on the Early American Frontier." In *Ritual Dynamics and the Science of Ritual*. Vol. 5: *Transfer and Spaces,* Gita Dharampal-Frick, Robert Langer, and Niles Holger Petersen, eds. Wiesbaden, Germany: Harrassowitz Books, 2010, pp. 171–88.

Pencak, William A., and Daniel K. Richter, eds. *Friends and Enemies in Penn's Woods: Indians, Colonists, and the*

Racial Construction of Pennsylvania. University Park, PA: Pennsylvania State University Press, 2004.

Plank, Geoffrey, *John Woolman's Path to the Peaceable Kingdom: A Quaker in the British Empire.* Philadelphia: University of Pennsylvania Press, 2012.

Preston, David L. *The Texture of Contact: European and Indian Settler Communities on the Frontiers of Iroquoia, 1667–1783.* Lincoln: University of Nebraska Press, 2009.

Richter, Daniel K. *Facing East from Indian Country: A Native History of Early America.* Cambridge: Harvard University Press, 2001.

Rhoades, Matthew L. *Long Knives and the Longhouse: Anglo-Iroquois Politics and the Expansion of Colonial Virginia.* Madison & Teaneck, NJ: Fairleigh Dickinson University Press, 2011.

Schwartz, Sally. *"A Mixed Multitude": The Struggle for Toleration in Colonial Pennsylvania.* New York & London: New York University Press, 1989.

Shannon, Timothy J. *Indians and Colonists at the Crossroads of Empire: The Albany Congress of 1754.* Ithaca, NY: Cornell University Press, 2002.

Shannon, Timothy J. "War, Diplomacy, and Culture: The Iroquois Experience in the Seven Years' War." In *Cultures in Conflict: The Seven Years' War in North America,* Warren R. Hofstra, ed. Lanham, MD.: Rowman & Littlefield, 2007, pp. 79–103.

Shoemaker, Nancy. "An Alliance Between Men: Gender Metaphors in Eighteenth-Century American Indian Diplomacy East of the Mississippi." *Ethnohistory* 46, no. 2 (spring 1999): 239–63.

Silver, Peter. *Our Savage Neighbors: How Indian War Transformed Early America.* New York: Norton, 2008.

Silverman, David J. *Thundersticks: Firearms and the Violent Transformation of Native America.* Cambridge & London: Belknap Press, 2016.

Spero, Patrick. *Frontier Country: The Politics of War in Early Pennsylvania.* Philadelphia: University of Pennsylvania Press, 2016.

Starna, William A. "The Diplomatic Career of Canasatego."In *Friends and Enemies in Penn's Woods: Indians, Colonists, and the Racial Construction of Pennsylvania,* in William A. Pencak and Daniel K. Richter, eds. University Park: Pennsylvania State University Press, 2004, pp. 144–63.

Wallace, Anthony F. C. *King of the Delawares: Teedyuscung, 1700–1763.* Syracuse, NY: Syracuse University Press, 1990.

Wainwright, Nicholas B. *George Croghan: Wilderness Diplomat.* Chapel Hill: University of North Carolina Press, 1959.

Ward, Matthew C. *Breaking the Backcountry: The Seven Years' War in Virginia and Pennsylvania, 1754–1765.* Pittsburgh: University of Pittsburgh Press, 2003.

Weslager, C. A. *The Delaware Indians: A History.* New Brunswick, NJ: Rutgers University Press, 1972.

PRIMARY SOURCES

Boyd, P., ed., *Indian Treaties Printed by Benjamin Franklin, 1736–1762.* Philadelphia: Historical Society of Pennsylvania, 1938.

Minutes of the Provincial Council of Pennsylvania. Vols. 6–7. Harrisburg, PA: T. Fenn, 1851.

Woolman, John. *The Journal and Essays of John Woolman.* Amelia Mott Gummere, ed. New York: Macmillan, 1922.

Zeisberger, David. *David Zeisberger's History of the Northern American Indians.* A. B. Hulbert and W. N. Schwarze, eds. Ohio State Archaeological and Historical Society, 1910.

ACKNOWLEDGMENTS

I deeply appreciate everyone who play-tested early versions of this game, especially those who offered advice, criticism, and direction. They include, but are not limited to, Mark Carnes, Lora Friedrich, Paul Fessler, Jace Weaver, Laura Weaver, Mark Higbee, P. Albert Lacson, Nancy Reagin, Stephen Feeley, Bill Offutt, Elly McConnell, and Bat Sparrow. I appreciate their determination to see the potential in what was, in retrospect, a bit of a mess.

I am particularly thankful for the early support extended to me by Mark Carnes and Dana Johnson of the Reacting consortium and my home institution, Simpson College, which allowed focused time for work on this project as part of a semester-length sabbatical leave.

As the game's development process proceeded, Linda Sinclair cheerfully transcribed a host of documents into digital form. She dealt with the odd spellings, eighteenth-century typography, and esoteric subject matter with aplomb and professionalism. I sincerely appreciate her efforts. Thanks also to Beriet Bichel for her work with early drafts of the maps.

As the manuscript neared completion, close readings by Paula Lazrus, Fred Hoxie, and Abby Markwyn, all yielded additional suggestions for clarification and improvement. Bill Bergmann made sure that I did not lapse in my attention to recent scholarship and guided my historical interpretations in a number of ways. Paul Otto gave the role sheets particular scrutiny, which yielded a number of important clarifications and the role assignment questionnaire. Thanks to them all, especially W. W. Norton's Scott Sugarman, Justin Cahill, Rachel Taylor, and the readers that they arranged to bring the game forward into its final form.

Finally, I appreciate all of the play-testers of various iterations of this game. Their willingness to grapple with this challenging and often sensitive material made the game what it is today.

APPENDICES : DELAWARE AS WOMEN

Historians differ about the exact meaning of making the Delaware "women." Historian C. A. Weslager provides a good overview of the first few rounds of this debate.[1]

There is no doubt that the Six Nations had relegated the Delawares to the position of women, and in this role the Delawares were prohibited from going to war or negotiating treaties. The questions that have been raised are concerned with when this occurred and whether the deprivation of masculine prerogatives was a result of conquest, as related by [Charles] Thomson, or whether the Delawares were somehow duped into accepting a role that they believed was an honored one but that brought them shame instead. According to this latter version, as told by the Moravian pastors Loskiel and Heckewelder, the Delawares agreed to accept what they believed was an honorable position among the Indian tribes as "peacemakers," a role played by some women of royal lineage among the Iroquois. Under this interpretation, as "matrons" in the society of Iroquois nations, the Delawares were delegated, by the Six Nations, the responsibility of negotiating peace between warring tribes. In this context, it is claimed, there was no shame attached to their being placed in the role of women and figuratively wearing petticoats. The weakness of this position is that there is absolutely no existing documentation wherein the Delawares were recognized as honored peacemakers, whereas there are numerous references to their being degraded to a shameful position as noncombatants.

I still hold to the view I first expressed in a paper in 1944, which has been reinforced by subsequent study, that the Delawares had been subjugated, and the Iroquois reduced them to a subservient position. In the circumstances the Delawares were placed in, there was no honor attached to being looked upon as women, rather they were humiliated because they were reminded constantly that they lacked political or military power. Canyase, a Mohawk, expressed it thus, "We, the Mohocks are Men; we are made so from above, but the Delawares are Women, and under our Protection, and of too low a kind to be Men."

Historian Jane Merritt presented a more dynamic view of this status—one in which the meaning of women *changed over time as a result of Indian action and changing metaphors.*[2]

In the mid-eighteenth century, the Six Nations claimed that they had conquered the Delawares and Shawnees in battle and conferred on them the metaphoric status of "women." According to historian Francis Jennings, the term originally meant that Delawares were "assigned a political role of neutrality so as to be able to assume the peacemaker's role when warring tribes wanted to end their strife without losing face." But in the treaty negotiations of the 1750s, the Delawares' status as women marked them as subordinate, not permitted to sell land or negotiate directly with the British. British

1. C. A. Weslager, *The Delaware Indians: A History* (New Brunswick, NJ: Rutgers University Press, 1972), pp. 180–81.

2. Jane T. Merritt, "Metaphor, Meaning, and Misunderstanding: Language and Power on the Pennsylvania Frontier," in *Contact Points: American Frontiers from the Mohawk Valley to the Mississippi, 1750–1830,* Andrew R. L. Clayton and Fredrika J. Teute, eds. (Chapel Hill: University of North Carolina Press, 1998): pp. 77, 79.

colonial governments, which had often been impatient with self-proclaimed or scattered native leaders in the Pennsylvania backcountry, welcomed this arrangement. By symbolically subordinating Delawares in the context of Indian-white relations, Pennsylvania could treat directly with an assumed political power, the Six Nations, who were much more cooperative when it came to selling land.

The term "women" as applied to Delawares was nominally based on the restricted public role of Indian women. Historically, Indian women enjoyed a certain degree of economic autonomy and control within native households and communities. They owned longhouses, controlled material and agricultural resources, and passed on property to their children. Native women also attended treaty conferences, often seated prominently according to their individual status, and advised the men, but they had limited power to speak in political forums. Their restricted public role, however, did not diminish their authority at home. Yet, despite their persuasive voice in the community and their presence in public, during the 1750s Iroquois, white, and Delaware men turned the concept of native women's authority on its head as a means of shaming and excluding men from places of power within the diplomatic arena.

This definition changed over time, partly as a result of dealing with Europeans in various treaty negotiations. This game is set in a period of considerable disagreement over the exact meaning of the metaphor. Merritt continues.

Apparently Indian diplomats felt the need to use specific European concepts of female gender, in which women could not own and sell land, to delineate Delawares' subordinate position in terms that Euramericans would clearly understand.

Indeed, by using gendered representations politically, Iroquois, Delawares, and Euramericans—men and women alike—began to change the meaning of the political category of "women." After the Delawares and Shawnees attacked the Pennsylvania and Virginia frontiers in 1755, the governors of both colonies begged the Six Nations to control the Delawares who were responsible. In January 1756, Robert Dinwiddie of Virginia told the Six Nations: "You looked upon [Delawares] as Women who wore petticoats; they never dar'd to do any thing of Importance without your leave, for they knew if they did you would Chastize them." If not punished, Delawares "will think themselves as good Men as you, and you will lose the name of being their Masters." In July, at Easton, Pennsylvania, the Six Nations again reminded Delawares; "You are our Women; our Fore-Fathers made you so, and put a Petticoat on you, and charged you to be true to us, and lie with no other Man; but of late you have suffered the String that tied your Petticoats to be cut loose by the French, and you lay with them, and so became a common Bawd, in which you acted very wrong, and deserve Chastisement." The Iroquois did not merely apply an alternative cultural category of femaleness in a political setting to convince whites to join them against Delawares. By the 1750s, Iroquois used these gendered representations to express the intimate and personal betrayal they felt as they wrestled to control Delawares.

Despite the use of these gendered images within a political arena, the Six Nations were not very successful in controlling their "women." Delawares, instead, exploited the same images in order to manipulate Englishmen and Iroquois. They decided where and when they would be women.[3]

Whatever the case, being called women appeared to bother the Delaware. It irritated Teedyuscung in particular. As his biographer, Anthony F. C. Wallace, notes.

3. This view is largely supported by David Zeisberger in *David Zeisberger's History of the Northern American Indians,* A. B. Hulbert and W. N. Schwarze, eds. (Ohio State Archaeological and Historical Society, 1910), pp. 34–36.

One of the things that Teedyuscung brooded about was being called a "woman" by the Six Nations. The word rankled, and the shame he felt on its account led him to the misconception (which his clerk, Charles Thomson, has embalmed in his famous *Alienation of the Delawares*) that the Six Nations' sole interest in the Delawares was to grind them into the dirt. * * * Technically, being "women" meant only that they were expected to entertain official emissaries from the Great Council with food and lodging. * * * The Delawares were also not given the privilege of speaking in the Great Council except on specific invitation; they were enjoined (as were all other subordinate adherents of the League) not to engage in irresponsible warfare. * * * But with the growth of bad feeling between the Delawares and the Iroquois after 1737, the "women" epithet began to come into use as a term of opprobrium, as an insulting nickname with which Six Nations speakers would taunt the down-and-out Delawares.[4]

4. Anthony F. C. Wallace, *King of the Delawares: Teedyuscung, 1700–1763* (Syracuse, NY: Syracuse University Press, 1990), p. 195.

APPENDICES : TEEDYUSCUNG'S RAID

Historian Anthony F. C. Wallace's account of Teedyuscung's raid into the Delaware Valley helps explain Delaware motives and tactics in their raids on the Pennsylvania frontier in the winter of 1755–56.[5]

The scalping raid was pretty much a family affair. Of the thirty warriors in Teedyuscung's party, three were sons of his (including Amos and Jacob), three were half-brothers (Sam Evans, Tom Evans, and Peter, alias Young Captain Harris, who had been baptized by the Moravians), and one was a nephew (Christian, the son of his half-brother Joe Evans). They reached the settlements north of the Kittatinnies, close by the Delaware, on New Year's Eve. No time was wasted. Teedyuscung and his three sons and their comrades quietly surrounded a party of four white men working in the fields of the Weeser plantation. The elder Weeser and Hans Adam Hess were suddenly shot down, and the two young men, Leonard and William Weeser, were seized by the Indians who rushed out of hiding. Amos, Teedyuscung's son, personally captured William and immediately handed him over to his father.

Next morning Teedyuscung, again leading his little band of warriors, descended on two other plantations in the neighborhood. At the farm of Peter Hess they killed Nicholas Burman and another hired hand, and captured Peter Hess and his elder son Henry. At nine o'clock they visited the place of Peter Hess's brother, where they killed Nicholas Coleman and a laborer named Gottlieb, and took prisoner Peter's brother and one other man. After firing the stables, burning the house and a barrack of wheat, and killing the cattle, most of the horses, and the sheep, they led off three horses and the prisoners northward over Second Mountain. At the Great Swamp they caught up with five of their party who had turned homeward the day before with the Weeser boys.

The Great Swamp was thirty miles from Weeser's, and old Peter Hess was failing, apparently, after the long walk. Rather than be burdened with a useless old man, they killed him, stabbing him to death, stripping off his clothes, and taking his scalp, while his son looked on helplessly. Then they went on [to Tioga in Iroquois country].

* * *

Teedyuscung never went out with a war party again. He had amassed sufficient honor from his one successful venture to assure his status as a sachem in fact if not in customary law. But this did not mean that he had laid down the hatchet. His function now was that of coordinator and "boss."

Historian C. A. Weslager sees vengeance as the primary motive for Delaware who took up the hatchet in 1755.[6]

When Shingas and his war captains from the Ohio launched their attacks—and when Captain Jachebus, Teedyuscung, and other Susquehanna Delaware captains took their braves on the warpath—it was with malice in their hearts and an obsession to destroy white people. This hatred caused them

5. Anthony F. C. Wallace, *King of the Delawares: Teedyuscung, 1700–1763* (Syracuse, NY: Syracuse University Press, 1990), pp. 83–84.

6. C. A. Weslager, *The Delaware Indians: A History* (New Brunswick, NJ: Rutgers University Press, 1972), pp. 230–31.

to inflict terrible atrocities on settlers of all nationalities and of all ages. No white family was safe, as warriors seemed to sweep down from nowhere with bloodcurdling war whoops, their faces and bodies covered with paint. They set fire to houses and barns, killed some residents, and took others into captivity. There was no single cause to which these attacks can be attributed; they were not designed to avenge a single incident like the Walking Purchase. It was a matter of retaliation against successive broken promises made over a period of years by Dutch, Swedes, and English—and against unscrupulous traders who cheated Delawares, debauched their people with rum, and took liberties with their squaws when their husbands were hunting in the woods. They were expressing a deep-seated hatred of white people who spread smallpox, contagious fevers, venereal diseases, and other ailments that decimated the Indian population. They were also flaunting in the faces of the Six Nations the folly of the myth that, since they had been figuratively emasculated, they must permanently play the undignified role of pacifistic women.

Despite the lack of an overall military strategy, some two hundred Delaware warriors living on the Susquehanna and seven hundred from the Ohio waged a commando war which was an orgy of bloodletting that marked the Delawares as brutal and ruthless warriors who showed no mercy.